Rereading Exodus along the Anacostia

Some Lessons of Cross River Dialogue

Virginia Avniel Spatz

Charnice Milton Community Bookstore
2022

www.weluvbooks.org

1918 Martin Luther King Jr. Avenue, SE

Washington, DC 20020

Charnice Milton Community Bookstore presents this title as part of an effort to promote literacy and crucial community conversations.

Charnice A. Milton, her memory is a blessing, was a local journalist for whom reading and writing were crucial. Books were refuge and companion throughout her life. As a journalist, Charnice used writing to serve the community in which she was raised. She was killed on her way home from assignment, and her homicide remains unsolved. She is missed.

Visit WeLuvBooks.org for more on the CMCB and on Charnice Milton (June 18, 1987 – May 27, 2015) herself.

ISBN 978-1-7344418-1-9 paperback
978-1-7344418-2-6 epub

Companion Volume:
Recounting Along the Exodus: 49 Stages from Narrow Place to What Next? Some Lessons of Cross River Dialogue (epub) ISBN: 978-1-7344418-3-3

Preface

Thank you for picking up this book. *Rereading Exodus* is a journey, and I appreciate everyone who takes even a few of its steps with me. This book uses Exodus narrative -- a story important to many aspects of popular culture -- as a tool for exploring power, oppression, and clashes of perspectives. The goal is to learn how we got into this "Narrow Place" of inequality, militarism, and racism and how we might get ourselves -- all of us -- out.

This book has been in process, in one form or another, since the Before Times. Back then, I fretted that some of what I wrote was too harsh, not "balanced" enough, or just too direct. Today, I am not sure there are words harsh enough for our country's lethal racial divides. I never deliberately share falsehoods or half-truths; at the same time, however, I recognize no "other side" on when it comes to denying anyone's humanity and human rights. As for over-directness, I recall a long-ago ballet teacher who told her classes: If you are timid in your presentation, I might miss a dangerous mistake. Whatever you're doing, do it all the way, and then we can work on corrections together.

...I have hesitated many times in sending this book out to the world. In some ways, the easier course would be to keep my words to myself...or hold out for perfection, its impossibility shielding me from ever finishing. But there are conversations we need to have, and work we need to do. Now. It is my fervent hope that this far-less-than-perfect offering will launch some necessary discussions.

It is not humblebrag to say I am sure there are mistakes in here. There will undoubtedly be typos and nonsense ahead -- for those I apologize and hope they are not too distracting. There will also be more serious missteps -- for those I hope readers will engage the concepts and let me know where future discussions need shifting, as well as advising me of errors or lack of clarity. -- Virginia in DC, March 29, 2022/26 Adar II 5782

"The story of Passover is a journey, and like most journeys,
it is taking much longer than it ought to take,
no matter how many times we stop and ask for directions."
– Lemony Snicket ("Playground") commentary, *New American Haggadah*

Table of Contents

This book includes an appendix offering a 49-stage thought-journey in conjunction with *Rereading Exodus* and for those who practice counting the Omer. Throughout the text, counting icons indicating a link to a learning focus and a ritual pause to bless and count.

1	2	3	4	5	6	7
8	9	#			13	14
15	16	links to		20	21
22	23	Omer		27	28
29	30	count		34	35
36	37			41	42
43	44	45	46	47	48	49

Also available as a separate volume,
Recounting Exodus along the Anacostia,
and in daily emails for Omer 5782: a set of daily pages, with a one-page learning focus, a special meditation for this journey, and the ritual blessing and count. Visit rereading4liberation.com for details.

When speaking of someone who has died,
there is a Jewish tradition of adding: *z"l.*
This is short for:
"zichrone livracha: may their memory be for a blessing"

It is this author's practice here to omit this expression
for historical personages
or for people who were strangers to me.
I do include it for those I knew or at least met.
Thus: Glen Ford (z"l) and Dick Gregory (z"l)
but just a name (and dates) for many others.

There are a few exceptions as noted.

DC, Washington, The District

This book is written from and about "DC," a city of some 700,000 people divided in several ways, as will be discussed throughout. One obvious division is the four quadrants: Northwest, Northeast, Southwest, and Southeast; another is in how this place is called.

"Washington" and "DC" sometimes occupy the same streets, meetings and grocery stores. But they are not identical places.

"Washington" is a city centered on the nation's capital, its work, and its links to folks "back home." Some Washington residents live here for years, even decades, maintaining connections with the state or Congressional district that sent them here.

The author interned in Washington for three weeks, between high school and college, and visited a few times before moving to town and from time to time afterward. She has friends who live and work there. She and her husband once considered moving to Washington; as things worked out, they have lived for going on 35 years and raised two children, now adults who each live elsewhere, in DC.

DC is an unusual place for many reasons, including our lack of statehood and direct Congressional interference in our budget and operations. The city is also affected by its status as the nation's capital and by ideas – sometimes shared by people who actually live and/or work here – that "no one is from here," that this is not a "real town," that the whole city is just a backdrop for the federal government. These points will arise, at times, on the journey ahead.

Note on language: "The District" is sometimes used here for the corporate entity or where "DC" alone is awkward, repetitive, or might be confused with other uses, like the comic book universe. "Columbus" rarely comes into the picture.

Preliminaries: What This Book Is, Is Not

A key element in the journey to liberation for all is seeking to understand the workings of oppression and our part in them. We cannot work effectively to end what we do not comprehend. And we cannot act effectively if we feel hopeless, ill-equipped, over-whelmed, and isolated. This book attempts to address these issues with a shared journey.

The Exodus story is a narrative central to religious and popular culture in the U.S. *Rereading Exodus along the Anacostia* links that story to my own struggles around liberation in my adopted hometown of DC and invites readers to join me in a journey along and across "the River" -- sometimes the Anacostia, sometimes the river of Pharaoh and Moses; sometimes both at once. Many things that DC has taught me about Exodus, and that Exodus teaches about life in this city, apply to other places as well. It is that learning journey

We must work to understand what it means to be in this "Narrow Place" and how we're going to get ourselves -- all of us – out.

Exodus is a valuable tool in this urgent work, which white folks, in particular, must undertake. And soon.

I hope to share. To clarify: what I can share is mostly a propensity for questions, a commitment to seeking new ways forward, and a sense of urgency taught by Exodus and by some experiences of intergroup dialogue.

Jews, especially white Jews, must explore our roles in DC's shifting power dynamics – and what better lens than the Exodus tale?

DC is a peculiar place for several reasons. One is its history as "Chocolate City" which has become "Chocolate Chip City," due to extreme demographic change: Eighty thousand Black people were displaced over the last 20 years, while a majority of newcomers are white,

and DC's Jewish population has roughly doubled. Of course, diversity of

DC (and Washington) is not entirely captured in "black and white." But these racializations and their intersection with Jewishness are central to *Rereading Exodus*.

The change from "Chocolate" to "Chips" requires careful reflection on shifting power dynamics. The big increase in DC's Jewish population means Jews in particular, especially white Jews, need to explore our roles in this city. But all who care about DC must work to understand what it means to be in this "Narrow Place" (more on this ahead) and how we're going to get ourselves -- all of us -- out.

Origins of the project -- This book was originally conceived, in the Before Times, as a project of the Cross River Dialogue, a small group of white Jews living west of the Anacostia River and Black non-Jews living or working east of the River. (The Potomac River might play a bigger role in some aspects of geography and history, and in some art forms, but it is not "the River" here.) This project has since shifted. *Rereading Exodus* in its current form is informed by my experience with CRD and gratefully shares some lessons learned. But this is not a group project.

This is not a group project. Opinions are the author's, unless noted. All mistakes are the author's, too.

Although not a group project, this book was formed in conversation with two Cross River Dialoguers who help me explore the needs of our city, intergroup politics and power. This book owes a great deal to Maurice Cook, executive director of Serve Your City DC/Ward 6 Mutual Aid, and to Kymone Freeman, co-owner of We Act Radio, colleague in the Charnice Milton Community Bookstore effort, and organizer of the Black LUV (Love.Unity.Vision) Festival. Nevertheless, I am responsible for all the content here, unless otherwise noted, and any errors are mine.

Another origin of this project is years of my own struggles around understanding "Exile" and its relationship to the Exodus narrative, to Diaspora Judaism -- Jewish thought and practice that lives in and celebrates wherever we are without relying on nationalism -- and to the application of the Exodus themes in community- and coalition-building.

We will be exploring an ancient story of oppression and liberation, rereading as we go for new ways forward. The main text is designed to require no particular exposure to any Jewish text or tradition and no particular background in DC history. Some material -- DC background and notes on Hebrew, plus related rants, however informative -- are offered in

The main text is designed to require no exposure to any Jewish text or tradition and no special background in DC history.

a variety of text boxes. This boxed material is meant to include readers of all backgrounds, without interfering with the main text. And it helps satisfy my own footnote-ish tendencies.

On the subject of footnotes and a warning -- This is as good a time as any to note that I have been reading and rereading Exodus for decades in all kinds of study and worship settings and on my own. I have read countless books and articles and joined Jewish education classes, but I am not formally trained as a scholar of Bible or Judaism. In addition, I have lived in DC a long time, participated in many ways and learned many things, but I am not a trained historian or expert on economics or legislation.

I am a journalist, with on-the-job training, and I am very careful in citing sources. I do not aim here, however, for exhaustive, authoritative, or "balanced" discussion on any topic. I hope that readers will accompany me on this journey and explore further on their own, perhaps using the citations provided. I do not pretend that I know "the way," but I do promise never to knowingly mislead....and I am grateful to everyone who joins me on this road. I look forward to hearing from others as we travel this challenging path together.

> **I do not aim here for exhaustive, authoritative, or "balanced" discussion on any topic.**

Race, Harm and Healing

The content of *Rereading Exodus along the Anacostia* is disturbing and will affect some readers more deeply than others, and it's important to begin this journey with acknowledging this. For anyone taught to aim for "color-blind" or "we're all equals" discussion, this book may seem overly direct and unnecessarily focused on race. For readers who live with the affects of structural and interpersonal racism every day, *Rereading Exodus* may seem to be stating the obvious or not direct enough.

Some of the lessons from our Cross River Dialogue are shared here, and authors more qualified than I to address harms of racism are cited throughout. As we begin, I rely on the work of Rhonda V. Magee for her insight on how race operates in our individual thinking and emotional lives, and for help in approaching these topics in a mindful way.

Rhonda Magee is a professor of law and trained in teaching mindfulness-based stress-reduction; she is also a Black woman with decades of experience operating in white-dominated spaces. Magee describes her life work as "dissolving the lies that racism whispers about who we really are, and doing whatever I can to reduce the terrible harm it causes us all" (p. 16, Magee, *The Inner Work of Racial Justice*).

The Inner Work of Racial Justice: Healing Ourselves and Transforming Our Communities through Mindfulness. Rhonda V. Magee. TarcherPerigee (Penguin Random House), 2019. The book is now available in paperback, ebook, and audio. The author's website includes her 2015 article, "The Way of ColorInsight," and additional free resources.

She begins her book with what she calls a "Race Story," a personal "reflection on race in American life." She urges a practice of mindfulness as a tool "for understanding our experiences around race and identity" and shares the following at the outset:

> Mindfulness is essential to developing the capacity to respond, rather than simply react as if on autopilot, to what we experience.
>
> To practice The Pause, you simply stop what you are doing and intentionally bring your awareness to the experience of the present moment... [see her book, "A Gentle Practice for Opening Up to Painful Emotions" on mindful.org, or just pause and notice]....
>
> Take a few minutes to write about what has come up for you during your Pause. This is especially important if you experienced strong emotions, or if some of your own memories or Race Stories emerged from their buried places. In my own experience, and as research has shown, even short periods of writing about emotionally difficult events in our past can assist us in deep healing.
>
> As you continue reading, engage in the loving awareness practice of The Pause whenever you need additional support.-- Magee, p.17-18

"As you continue reading" above is addressed to readers of *The Inner Work of Racial Justice*. But the same advice applies here.

Magee's work has been enormous help to me, and she will be quoted a number of times later in this book. I highly recommend checking out her book and/or other resources available on-line.

Bible, Harm and Healing

Rereading Exodus makes use of biblical text as well as commentaries from Jewish, and occasionally Christian or other religious, traditions. The purpose of this work is learning and repair. But it must be acknowledged that we are participating in a system that was not designed for most of us and has, over centuries and in the lifetimes of readers, caused a great deal of harm, to some of us more than others. In particular, Bible and racial injustice are inextricably linked.

Many Bible readers, of many traditions, work to transform what we have inherited into something that supports our whole community and globe.

We do not stop wrestling our sacred texts for a blessing, demanding from them a way toward Liberation for all. But the author wishes to recognize that approaching the Bible at all can be more of an effort for some of us.

If working on this book in a group, please keep in mind differences in participant background, in terms of Bible and the general topics raised here.

Hebrew Bible, *Tanakh,* consists of 24 books, 39 in translation (two each of Kings, Samuel, and Chronicles and 12 separate books in place of one Hebrew "Minor Prophets"). The first five books are "*Torah* [Teaching]," also called "*Chumash*" or "Pentateuch," from Hebrew and Latin for five. After Torah, *Nevi'im* proceeds through narrative around the Land and further prophetic readings. *Ketuvim* includes Psalms, Ecclesiastes, and other writings. The last book, Chronicles, ends with Babylonian Captivity (586 BCE), the final two verses relating Persia's King Cyrus promising return.

TaNaKH = *Torah* + *Nevi'im* [Prophets] + *Ketuvim* [Writings]

General Format

At its heart, this book is about the journey away from enslavement in *Mitzrayim,* the biblical Egypt, and toward Revelation. It does not assume any particular orientation to the calendar or to Judaism, and it is designed to be accessible to readers from any background who are interested in liberation and the Exodus framing.

An appendix offers material for those who follow the *Sefira,* the period of "counting," between Passover and Shavuot (in the same calendar and thematic space as the Christian Pentecost) or who wish to take a 49-step journey at any time. This can also be used to prepare for Passover or for upcoming elections, for example. But it need not be read in any particular timeframe.

The pace and path of the journey are flexible:

> Skim. Binge. Delve.
> Pursue one stage per day or one chapter per week.
> Follow up on every citation to learn more.
> Select just a few to digest and discuss, maybe meditate.
> Work alone or in a group.

However you explore this Exodus journey, find ways to act.

God, Quotations, Translations

Names for God are an important part of this journey and discussed along the way. Bible text in Hebrew uses a number of different names for God, all conjugated as masculine and using "he" pronouns. Bible translations into

English have adopted many strategies for avoiding obviously masculine language for God, sometimes leaving the Hebrew names untranslated. But there is still no common practice around this.

Bible translations shared here are, unless otherwise noted, slightly adapted versions of the public domain "Old JPS" (Jewish Publication Society 1917). In addition to adapting gendered God-language, old-fashioned locutions, like "thou hast," are updated. In classical sources, or within another author's work, any biblical quotations are left as is, unless noted, and there is no attempt to rewrite gendered language or old-fashioned spelling and wording in most older commentaries.

I relied on Mechon-Mamre.org for basic Bible translations. This is a very handy source with easy-to-access Hebrew and public domain English as well as some other material. I also use BibleHub.com, a Christian site with powerful interactive tools including a built-in biblical Hebrew dictionary and concordance, as well as Sefaria.org, a Jewish with a wealth of resources.

Language and "Thematic Elements"

As noted above, anyone taught to aim for "color-blind" or "we're all equals" discussion might find *Rereading Exodus* overly direct and unnecessarily focused on race. Addressing racial inequities requires focusing on race and color, and other topics including wealth and power, in ways that are uncomfortable for some people, especially those of us whose privilege permits us to avoid these topics when it suits us.

There are many "thematic elements" in *Rereading Exodus* that could be upsetting to some readers for many reasons. Part of

> Sometimes young adult fiction says it all:
>
> > Edith Grayston: Politics doesn't interest you. Why?
> > Sherlock Holmes: Because it's fatally boring.
> > Grayston: Because you have no interest in changing a world that suits you so well.
> > -- *Enola Holmes* (Netflix 2020, Harry Bradbeer, director; scene is 60 minutes into the show)
>
> It is 1884, London. Sherlock is a white man with wealth enough to work as a detecting consultant only when he chooses (and, in this story, mediating between older brother Mycroft and younger sister Enola and their mother, who is supporting Reform along with Edith); Edith is a Black woman running a shop, offering revolutionary reading material to her customers, and teaching martial arts to women.
>
> > One who says: "What concern are the problems of the community to me?" helps to destroy the world.
> > – *Midrash Tanchuma Mishpatim 2*

the work of collaboration- and community-building is learning to commu-nicate so as to move into challenging territory in ways that disturb those used to more than our share of comfort and foster comfort in those too used to the opposite.

Black and white: In general this book follows Associated Press style (up-dated in early 2021) on "Black" as an identity and "black" as a color, while "white" remains lowercase except as part of a proper noun. Many related expressions are discussed as they arise. Usage in quotations is usually main-tained as is.

Jew and anti-Jewish: "Jew" encompasses many backgrounds and histories, although common usage in the U.S. frequently employs the term as short-hand for "Jew of European descent and Ashkenazi tradition." Sometimes avoiding this assumption means overly wordy or awkward language; apolo-gies. When speaking of a particular experience of Judaism or identity within Jewish communities, the expression "Jew of Color" is sometimes used, along with the more specific "Black and Jewish" or "Black Jew." BI-POC or BIJOC (Black, Indigenous, and Person/Jew of Color) is used in some contexts. Usage in quotations is maintained as is, except as noted.

In my own writing, I use "anti-Jewish" and "anti-Jewishness" rather than "antisemitic" and "antisemitism" (see box for related history). I do not, however, change language in quotations from other sources. This may be confusing, but perhaps that confusion can help us re-think what it is that we are talking about, anyway, and and why.

Antisemitic and Anti-Jewish

Although anti-Jewish ideas and action are far older, the word "antisemite" is dated to 1879, attributed to German politician Wilhelm Marr (1819-1904), who founded the *Antisemitenbund* [League of Antisemites]. This group advocated legal separation of Jews and non-Jews, expulsion of Jews who arrived after 1914, ban of Jews from public office, professions, land ownership, and other rights. (Source: US Holocaust Memorial Museum)

More Background: A Few Demographic Details for DC, Beyond

Jews -- roughly 7.1 million of us -- make up about 2.2% of the United States population and far less than 1% percent (0.19%) worldwide.

The Washington Metropolitan Area -- sometimes called "DMV" these days, i.e., District, suburban Maryland, and northern Virginia -- now has the third largest Jewish population in the country, tied with Chicago at just shy of 300,000; far behind New York's two million plus, and about half of LA's

622,000 (2020 stats, source: *The American Jewish Year Book, 2021*, by Sheskin & Dashefsky via Jewish Virtual Library).

Inside DC proper, Jews are still a small minority. However, the Jewish population has grown from about 28,000 a few years ago to roughly 57,000. This is a jump from 5% to 8% of the city's 700,000 residents. (Sources: World Population Review and Pew Research studies)

Further details are not easy to find or consistent in terms of study methodology. How Jews of Color are identified is particularly contested: results vary from 5 or 6% to 10-15% and with many studies not gathering this data at all.

There is no specific data on Jews of Color in DC, while statistics used to count DC's Black, white, Hispanic/Latinx, Asian, American Indian, and Native Hawaiian populations -- as defined by the U.S. Census -- do not tell us who is or is not identified as a Jew. The Black population of DC (no doubt, some Jews among them) dropped by 80,000 over the first two decades of the 21st Century.

Image: view of DC's Sousa Bridge, spanning the Anacostia River, from the east bank. Flowering bush in the foreground, with river and bridge behind; surface and highway directional signs atop bridge visible, but vantage point is too low to show any vehicular or pedestrian traffic on Pennsylvania Avenue SE crossing the bridge.

Many things that DC has taught me about Exodus, and that Exodus teaches about life in this city, apply to other places as well.

Starting Points

The Book of Exodus starts with individuals showing up in a place that is new to them. This is not insignificant. Much of *Rereading Exodus* is about what happens -- to a place and its people -- when new folks arrive. It is also about the more usual view of Exodus as a story of getting out.

מצרים *Mitzrayim*

In English, the Book of Exodus takes place in "Egypt." *Rereading Exodus* uses a transliteration of the Hebrew word, *"Mitzrayim,"* instead, to keep the biblical place – and its symbolic meanings – distinct from any actual country, ancient or contemporary. *"Mitzrayim"* can reference the land or a collective people/nation.

Similarly, a Hebrew transliteration, *"Yisrael,"* is used to distinguish biblical from other usage. In Bible discussed here, it is both another name for Jacob and the name of a people. (At this point in the biblical story there is no place of this name. In instances where the historical or contemporary nation is meant, "Israel" is used.)

"Yisrael-ite" is used for an individual or the adjective form. This book uses an invented parallel term, *"Mitzrayim-ite,"* (rather than "Egyptian") for individuals and the related adjective.

Unless otherwise noted, original language is maintained in quotations.

To truly conceive, what it would mean to escape "the Narrow Place" of the Exodus story we must first explore how all the parties ended up in here and how we/they relate to one another.

צר *Tzar*

The Hebrew "*tzar*" means "narrow" and the plural "*tzarim*" is "narrow straits." So, based on Hebrew wordplay, *The Zohar* (a mystical work from 13th Century Spain) suggests that the Exodus story is about escaping from our own "narrow places." Centuries of later Jewish teaching elaborated themes of leaving behind constricted views and narrow-mindedness.

Locating Ourselves

Note that "we" *and* "they" are "in here," this Narrow Place.

They. On the one hand, we are exploring characters in a story that comes to us via the Book of Exodus, which is set at least 2500 years ago. From that perspective, *Mitzrayim-ites* and *Yisrael-ites,* as collectives, and individuals, including Moses and Pharaoh and the midwives and the taskmasters, are all "they." Perhaps we resemble one or more characters or identify with a whole people in the tale, even imagine what it might be like to live through the Exodus narrative as one of "them." But they're still not exactly us.

Versions of the story have also come to us through movies and books and other art forms over the centuries. Those interpretations provide different perspectives on what "they" of Exodus do and feel, and we might identify with or resemble them as well. But we are still readers or viewers or listeners outside the narrative situation of the art, usually long ago and far away.

We. At the same time, it is a common Jewish practice to read the Torah from inside the story: It is happening to "us" right now, with "us" understood in many ways, depending on the interpretation. This is particularly true of the Exodus story, which Jews are told we must understand in each generation as though we ourselves experienced rescue from *Mitzrayim.*

Crucial Note:

The Exodus is an important part of theology for Jews
and for Christians.
***Rereading Exodus* is NOT about any religious community's understanding of covenant.**
It's about the story,
"theirs" – as in the characters we read about in the Bible –
and "ours," as in what lessons we learn from the story for ourselves and our communities.

...Note: "we" in the previous sentence means "Jews." In addition, my "we" is sometimes DC's people or participants in the Cross River Dialogue or another collective of which I'm part. I also use "we" for "you and me" as we read together on this *Rereading Exodus* journey.

Of course, the first-person plural is a language feature most of us navigate regularly without much thought. But figuring out who "we" are at any given point is an important part of this book's journey, and it's a crucial part of intergroup effort, from "Dialogue" to collaboration building....

I. I personally am just as conscious of being firmly inside *Mitzrayim*, trying to understand who is in here with me and how we might get ourselves out, as I am aware of sitting a mile from the Anacostia River trying to puzzle out who are the parties around me, how we relate well and not-so-well to each other, and how we might move ourselves toward Liberation for all.

Us. Even if this way of reading is strange to you, I invite you to join me in this trip, beginning simultaneously

- on the banks of "The River" in the biblical Narrow Place,

- on the banks of the River here in DC, and

- in your own location, with its narrowness and its possibilities.

As we go along, there will be many opportunities to (re-)consider

- who we are in the Bible tale we're exploring;

- who we are in the story unfolding around our physical residence -- geographically, politically, socially;

- and who we are as individuals with a variety of identities.

This book shares elements of my own journeys through the Exodus text, in the context of cross-community work here in DC, and it presents some specific tools to support this effort. Please use what is helpful and discard the rest...and/or let me know where the journey went wrong and might profitably try a new path.

One of our starting points is ourselves. Fuzziness on our own identities and assumptions can unduly complicate our travels, for ourselves and others.

Clarifying Tools

Several years ago, I happened upon a "Bible Readers' Self-Inventory," in *People's Companion to the Bible* (see box). The inventory is a set of questions about both social location and orientation to biblical text. The former includes basics like family background, race, ethnicity, class, and education -- which are not always so "basic" to answer. The latter looks at ideas about communal standards and authority in teaching, exposure to Bible and development of ethics; this includes assumptions many of us received, however haphazardly, in childhood and have never been prompted to examine.

Factors in our social location influence how we read anything, including the Bible. Approaching Bible, in particular, often brings along strong feelings about how the text, or some of its interpretations, appeared in our personal lives: maybe as source of judgment and harm; maybe as newfound or lifelong comfort; maybe something in between or largely irrelevant for us. Bible also comes to us with its history of use in colonization and oppression as well as a source of cultural development, for better or worse.

The Peoples' Companion to the Bible (Fortress Press, 2010) aims to put "cultural diversity at the very center of reading the Bible." The Introduction alone (free PDF on their website) is a useful resource and includes the "self-inventory" for Bible readers.

Their self-inventory is designed for Christian readers, especially seminary students, so all the questions will not suit everyone. In particular, Jewish experience is not an exact fit, so I adapted it for myself and others. "Toward a Jews' Self-Inventory for Bible Readers," is available on "A Song Every Day" blog and at Academia.edu. Neither may suit you exactly, but at least some of the questions will likely be useful to every reader.

I could have told you most of that before I encountered the "Bible Readers' Self-Inventory."

Until I did, though, I had not really paused to think in careful detail about how my own background actively influences my Bible study and teaching, from my knee-jerk reactions to some male-centered language to deep concern over treating particular expressions of Judaism as "authoritative." Prior to working through the self-inventory, I don't remember consciously examining how my own economic circumstances, and changes in those over the years, might be affecting my reading.

Some of us have more experience than others in considering the basics of our social location in general:

> Readers who enjoy certain privileges in society—because of wealth, education, ethnicity, gender, sexual orientation, or other factors— may find themselves thinking that these factors "don't matter" for them as much as they might for others. If a [factor] seems unimportant or irrelevant, one might well ask *why?*
> -- Neal Elliott, *Peoples' Companion to the Bible* (Fortress, 2010 xxix)

Learning to be more explicit for myself, and able to articulate to others, where I'm coming from in Bible study has been illuminating for me. And I have found that the exercise made me more conscious of what I am bringing when I show up anywhere.

I highly recommend trying such an inventory or finding another way to explore location questions. Failing to recognize and name some of our basic assumptions can lead to confusion and undo conflict. Conversely, finding ways to identify our perspectives and bring them clearly to others helps expand horizons for everyone and contributes to deeper, stronger communities.

Another powerful resource is *The Inner Work of Racial Justice: Healing Ourselves and Transforming Our Communities through Mindfulness* (see box). Author Rhonda V. Magee hopes that working through this book will offer "space to become less reactive and to choose how we respond to injustice."

Us. Them. Me

As mentioned above, Exodus opens with some individuals showing up in a place that is new to them:

> Now these are the names of the sons of *Yisrael*, who came into *Mitzrayim* with Jacob; every man came with his household:
> -- Exodus 1:1

Here are a few questions to ponder as we begin to approach the text:

> Do we identify with the new arrivals or those already living in the place?
> Have we been taught to consider one group as "our people"?
> What were we taught about the other group?
> Who gets mentioned and who is named?

It is within my lifetime, and only after years of feminist/womanist Bible teaching and scholarship, that it became common to note that "these are the names" includes only men, to wonder about those not mentioned, and to realize how quickly the few women in Exodus disappear from the story. It is still far less common to recognize that some gender expressions and sexualities are not reflected at all in the Bible or in most Bible teaching.

The Book of Exodus is already richer and deeper than the one available when I was a child. Queer and other perspectives that used to be kept at the margins, if given space on the page at all, have already changed the shape of the text. But we are still in a Narrow Place in many aspects of our reading and have much work yet to do.

Example and Disclosure: Completing a Bible self-inventory was clarifying for me. I highly recommend giving it a try and share brief excerpts from my own as an example and to offer a few more details about how I approach Bible. As the *Peoples' Companion* reminds us: "...whether we are approaching it for the first time or have read it often.... none of us comes to the Bible as a 'blank slate.'"

Bible Self-Inventory Excerpts

I read as a woman valuing all gender expressions, egalitarianism, social justice, Judaism beyond borders, and cross-community understanding.

Bible wasn't a big influence in my earliest years; from age 11-ish, I learned that my own readings set me outside the community in which I was raised and that being a girl limited my options for influencing that community. Many years later, I found my way into Bible through female and other characters at the margins and through teaching stressing transformative possibilities.

More Generally: My upbringing includes the snobbery of "regular folks" toward the better-heeled; cis-het privileges as well as confusion and anger of a woman in a patriarchal religious world; benefits and challenges of growing up white on Chicago's West Side, with an enriching and relatively violence-free youth, followed by huge upheaval of the '60s, Urban Renewal, White Flight, and the complete dismantling of my childhood neighborhood.

Now, I try to prioritize sources, for study and citation, that affirm my values while also seeking variety in viewpoints.

The First Episode

In Hebrew, "Exodus" is known as "*Shemot* [Names]," and it begins:

> Now these are the names [*shemot*] of the sons of *Yisrael*,
> who came into *Mitzrayim* with Jacob;
> every man came with his household:
> Reuben, Simeon, Levi, and Judah;
> Issachar, Zebulun, and Benjamin;
> Dan and Naphtali, Gad and Asher.
> Altogether there were seventy persons of Jacob's issue;
> and Joseph was in Egypt already.
> -- Exodus 1:1-5

The first lines assume we already know a lot: Who is *Yisrael*? Where were his sons before? Why did they go into *Mitzrayim*? Is this story only about men? And who is Jacob?

...Supposing we already know that Jacob and *Yisrael* are two names for the same person, that raises a different question: Why is the text using both names?....

We can plow ahead in the story, even if we're feeling like we tuned in late or are getting the wrong reel of a movie (not that most devices are tuned these days or movies distributed in reels). We might wish for a hint, like the one opening *The Adventures of Huckleberry Finn:* "You don't know about me without you have read a book by the name of The Adventures of Tom Sawyer; but that ain't no matter" (Mark Twain, 1885). Maybe we just assume these verses reference a previous narrative installment and seek that out.

Names

Books of the Torah and weekly readings, "portions," are titled in Hebrew by their first distinct word. The book known in English as "Genesis" is called "*Breishit* [In the Beginning]" in Hebrew. The Book of Exodus is called "*Shemot* [Names]" in Hebrew, as is the first weekly portion in the book.

How might the title we use affect how we read the book?

Where to begin reading or studying is one important decision. Where a story starts is crucial to its telling.

Think of playmates explaining to their adult "who started it." Consider a public official announcing the decision not to run for re-election or a restaurant closing for the last time: A political journalist might start these tales at one point and a business reporter at another, while an oral storyteller might make a third choice. There isn't one clear "START" for all purposes.

Part of the work of *Rereading Exodus,* or Torah exploration more generally, is to add layers of experiences and perspectives to each aspect of the story.

Getting used to doing this is a tool we can also apply to many situations in our daily lives. And figuring out where a story does, or should, start is one element of that work. See below for two disturbing but crucial examples.

As *Rereading Exodus* continues we will take a sort of traveling-cartography approach, stepping back into the Book of Genesis and looking ahead to later books of Torah, to figure out where we are and add details as we go along. We will also be gathering material from our current circumstances to add to the mix. It is my fervent hope that exploring Exodus will help illuminate life in DC -- and/or wherever you are at the moment -- especially in terms of cross-community understanding. And vice versa.

Where does the story of a killing by police start?

Consider how we report violence, especially killings, by police officers. Where we start the telling has a great influence on how we understand what happened and this, in turn, has lasting implications for policy and other consequences....as well as for our own orientations in the universe.

Deon Kay, RIP

Consider the shooting death of 18-year-old Deon Kay (9/2/20) by DC's MPD (Metropolitan Police Dept): Do we start that story with MPD reporting a justified fatal shot? With reports of the officers' earlier actions? With young Deon's life?

We could start instead with what the DC Auditor called the "entirely improvised" and "reckless" approach of the officers (Office of DC Auditor: *The Metropolitan Police Department and the Use of Deadly Force: The Deon Kay Case.* 5/25/21) Or we could take a wider look at use of force in MPD, officer training, supervision, etc.

We could start with legal analyses of the relatively new DC Justice Lab or reports from the older policy groups, Stop Police Terror Project DC or Black Lives Matter DC. Or, should we step back further and begin where Kelly Brown Douglas does in *Stand Your Ground: Black Bodies and the Justice of God* (Orbis, 2015)?

For the record: I did not know Deon Kay personally, but I know people who did. I know others who join me in mourning this young life cut short and all of our failures, as adults responsible for the safety of our youth.

May his memory be for a blessing.

Where does the story of a hostage situation start?

Colleyville, TX is not geographically near DC, but the hostage situation that took place there reverberated along the Anacostia. And, while there is no DC Auditor's analysis or similar document to reference, there were affects in DC, and we can profitably consider how this story was reported.

Congregation Beth Israel, 1/15/22

Do we start with police and FBI sources outside, saying "hostages rescued"? Or do we begin with the story from inside, describing an escape without external intervention?

Does the story start with R' Charlie Cytron-Walker's decision to value hospitality and allow a cold stranger inside the synagogue?

Does it maybe start with this history?

> [The suspect] chose a Jewish synagogue, because he thought that Jews control the world. He thought that he could take Jews hostage, call up an influential rabbi** and she would snap her fingers and give him what he wanted. He truly believed that Jews control the media, that Jews control the government, that Jews control everything.
>
> ...Over the centuries entire Jewish communities have been destroyed because people believed that Jews drank the blood of non-Jewish children. Entire Jewish communities have been destroyed because people believed that Jews wanted to torture communion wafers. Entire Jewish communities have been destroyed because people believed that Jews were responsible for all the bad things in life – that we are the root of all evil.
>
> ...Far too many Jews have died because of it. This isn't distant history. This is a month ago. – R' Cytron-Walker, 2/17/22 testimony U.S. House Subcmt. on Crime, Terrorism, and Homeland Security

**Does the story start with the career of R' Angela Buchdahl, prominent rabbi (and one of the country's most prominent rabbis of color), and how the alleged perpetrator came to think her in charge of what he wanted?

Does it start with the individual who admits that, a few days before the incident, he sold a stolen, semiautomatic weapon to the suspected gunman, who claimed to need it for intimidation to settle a debt? Or with a judicial system that can make this Black man the face of an anti-Jewish hate crime/act of terrorism that he did not commit?

See also: R' Buchdahl. "Captives of Hope," 1/21/22 sermon, Central Synagogue (NYC). AP/Fort Worth Star Telegram, 2/17/22.

Getting Out, Getting Somewhere

In addition to the starting point, another crucial map element for a journey is its end: Sometimes the whole point is to get out; sometimes the journey has a pre-determined a destination; and sometimes the aim is the journey itself. The Exodus story can be read with all three end-points in mind:

- Much of the drama, in popular tellings and in the Bible itself, and Narrow Place;

- Early in the Exodus tale, Moses is told that God has a "better place" destination in mind, while the Genesis prequel suggests a sense of returning home as well; and

- The Jewish calendar sends us on a journey that keeps us wandering in the wilderness for much of the year.

Getting Out

Getting away from oppression in *Mitzrayim* is the climax of an epic full of promises, plagues, and politics. We might picture the story as told in Zora Neale Hurston's *Moses, Man of the Mountain* (1939), Cecil B. DeMille's *The Ten Commandments* (1956), or DreamWorks' *The Prince of Egypt* (1998). Or perhaps we rely on other artistic renderings, biblical teachings and/or Passover tellings. Whatever our sources, escape from *Mitzrayim* is dramatic and often treated as decisive and final:

> Oppression behind us;
> freedom ahead;
> halleluyah!
> And, on Passover: "Let's eat."

The story is longer and messier than we sometimes remember, however, and not nearly as final. Even after the crossing of the Sea of Reeds, there are 27 more chapters of Exodus and then the next three books of the Bible, all in the wilderness. The Torah closes, forty years on, an entire generation having perished on the journey and a river still to cross.

Hurston describes this moment from the perspective of Moses, at the end of his work and life:

> But here was Israel at the Jordan. If he had failed in his highest dreams he had succeeded in others. Perhaps he had not failed so miserably as he sometimes felt. Israel was at the Jordan inside as well as out.
> -- Hurston, *Moses, Man of the Mountain,* p.283

The leader is aware, in Hurston's telling as in many commentaries, of the ongoing trauma of *Mitzrayim*, the many who never made it out, the cost of the trek and the price still to be paid.

Still a Wilderness

Readers in 1939 were expected to see parallels between the ancient drama and both Black experience in the U.S. and the rise of Nazism worldwide. Eighty years after Hurston's writing, some dynamics she described continue to apply.

National leaders, not unlike Pharaoh, seek war abroad while declaring "We don't have any home problems that I can see" (*Moses*, p.62), for example. And with Facism again (or still) on the rise, we have much work to do toward understanding race and how it works in our overlapping Jewish and Black contexts.

Alicia Suskin Ostriker described the post-Exodus wilderness situation this way:

> ...The promised land really exists, it really doesn't, are we there yet. Borders unspecified, we will know when we've arrived....
>
> An impossible place, let freedom ring in it. We've been to the mountain. We've seen the land: A terrain of the imagination, its hills skipping for joy. How long, we say, we know our failure in advance, nobody alive will set foot in it.
> -- Ostriker, "The Nursing Father," *Nakedness of the Fathers*

We know our failure in advance. And yet.... We learn together. We build community. We celebrate. And we set off one more time, reaching toward a fuller future Redemption.

A Better Place?

In the annual Torah cycle, governing the Jewish calendar for centuries, we begin each Autumn reading of Creation and early ancestors, move through Exodus, then the wilderness and its Revelation, toward the Promised Land. We never get closer than the river bank opposite, though, hopeful but not yet home. Although later books of the Hebrew Bible follow *Yisrael* into the Land, the Torah cycle rewinds every year to "In the beginning."

This circular path is reflected in other aspects of Jewish thought and practice, including themes of the weekly sabbath and the annual festival cycle. Every spring, the festival cycle brings us back into Pharaoh's clutches, and centuries of teachers have considered ways to approach Passover's release....

...a tale we are we are commanded to remember, re-tell, and celebrate, even as we already know what is on the other side: Forty years of wandering that follow crossing of the Sea; Babylon captivity; and more loss and exile....

The circularity might suggest that we are perpetually trapped. But cycles also bring new opportunities.

We can show up better prepared.
We can bring new resources, friends, and colleagues..
We can approach perennial challenges with fresh energy.....
We can look at the Exodus narrative new this time.

Decades ago, Michael Walzer concluded *Exodus and Revolution* with this adage about "what the Exodus first taught" --

> -- first, that wherever you are, it is probably [*Mitzrayim*]
>
> -- second, that there is a better place, a world more attractive, a promised land;
>
> -- and third, that the way to the land is through the wilderness. There is no way to get from here to there except by joining together and marching.

There is much inspiration in this oft-quoted image of "joining together and marching" to that "better place." What was once an urgent call of Liberation Theology, however, has become a kind of platitude. And we are so easily lulled into thinking that we are moving toward a "better place" when, in reality, we've long since reconciled to marching in place.

Perhaps marching as a metaphor for liberation is experiencing a "crash"?

When a Story Crashes
Rabbi Benay Lappe, of SVARA: The Traditionally Radical Yeshiva, teaches that there are three options in the crash of a "master story" -- like ancient Judaism's organization around temple worship in Jerusalem:

1) re-entrench, ignore evidence of dysfunction: For example: there was already a drift away from Temple service even before the destruction in 70 CE; but responses included forms of "Nothing to see here," and then, "All will soon be as before."

2) choose a new story: post-Temple Jews could take up Greek, Roman or Christian stories, e.g.

3) transform the old story.

The last was pursued by Rabbis of the Mishnah, who created what we now know and practice, in many forms, as "(Rabbinic) Judaism" today.

Visit svara.org/crash/ to hear the "crash talk"

....The Exodus story -- as sometimes employed in Judaism, in some Liberation Theologies, and in a variety of artistic works -- is a definitive parting of oppressor and oppressed peoples. This has powerful uses.

But it also has limitations, especially when Passover participants are aware of our resemblance, individually and collectively, to Pharaoh. And such readings do not lend themselves to envisioning collaborative, joint liberation. For some of us, this represents a "crash" of sorts. But centuries of alternative, frequently more complex, readings offer possibilities for transforming the old story to serve post-Crash....

In many of our communities today -- here in DC, is one example -- displacement is a serious form of oppression, with imminent harm for people of color. At the same time, fear of displacement -- by refugees, Jews, Muslims, "them" -- fuels hatred, harsh laws, and violence in our country and beyond. Envisioning *en masse* departure of the oppressed may not be the most helpful metaphor for these circumstances. Maybe sticking around is the more liberatory choice, after all?

At the very least, we must ask some tough questions, of ourselves and our communities, about this concept of marching:

> Are we prepared to head toward something truly different?

> Will we let go of what we have in order to get there?

> With whom have we joined hands? Whom have we left behind?

> Have we been marching toward a liberation
> that never seems to materialize
> for so long that we now wonder if it's worth the upheaval?

Always a Turning Point?

In a long-ago discussion group, someone cited a Bible commentary that hinged on a "turning point," a precarious moment centered between the ten generations leading to that point and the ten to come. Another participant laughed, insisting that all moments -- in- or outside the Bible -- are between what came before and what comes after, that each moment is a "turning point" between one thing and another.

There's a similar scene in the movie "Little Man Tate" (Orion 1991; Jodie Foster, director): Six-year-old Fred Tate is in his elementary school classroom and clearly bored. The teacher writes on the chalkboard a series of whole numbers -- 1, 2, 3, 4, 5, 6... -- and asks: "Which of these numbers can be divided by two?" When no one responds, she calls hopefully on Tate, who responds flatly: "All of them."

The exact commentary in discussion of turning points is lost to me now, and the Sages' fondness for "tens" leaves many candidates. But here is an oft-quoted passage:

> [There were] ten generations from Adam to Noah, in order to make known what long-suffering is His; for all those generations kept on provoking Him, until He brought upon them the waters of the flood.

> [There were] ten generations from Noah to Abraham, in order to make known what long-suffering is His; for all those generations kept on provoking Him, until Abraham, came and received the reward of all of them. -- Pirkei Avot 5:2

The fictional young genius and my mathematically-focused friend are both correct, of course: Any number can be divided by any other (non-zero) number, and we can view all moments as the center of some timeline. Similarly, if the People always have a Narrow Place to escape, a wilderness to traverse, and a river to cross, we might simply declare: We're born, we wander, we reach the journey's apparent end -- what more is there to say?

Like young Tate, we may be impatient with what can seem limited perspectives. Like my discussion partner, we may find ourselves questioning the validity of some approaches to the text. If we're not careful, though, what was essential -- properties of odd and even numbers; theological implications of biblical structure -- can disappear from view.

Similarly, we already know the big sweeping views of Exodus, like "the main thing is to head toward what looks like justice," or "God is on the side of the beleaguered," etc. To really learn new lessons from Exodus we have to look very closely at both the text and the challenges we face today, exploring where they inform one another.

And, yes, we are always at a turning point. A good thing, too!

Because we need a new way forward.

The weight of this particular moment -- whenever we're encountering the Exodus text together -- should never be diminished. This is the one moment we have to act. And if we do not, the consequences will be dire for many.

Passover and Exodus

The Exodus story is linked in Jewish thought and practice to the festival of Passover -- *Pesach* in Hebrew. The festival, detailed in the Book of Exodus, is observed for seven or eight days in different Jewish traditions. The first night (or two) is marked with a Passover *Seder* ["order"] ritual, structured around four cups of wine, special foods, and storytelling. Each cup is associated with a different verb (explored later).

The storytelling is based on "the *Haggadah*," from the Hebrew for "telling." Central to most such texts (plural: *haggadot*) are some elements that were fixed about 2000 years ago -- although fixed somewhat differently in different strands of tradition – plus biblical passages, songs and readings added over the centuries. In addition to Exodus selections, "the telling" includes parts of Genesis and later books of the Bible. What is incorporated can differ enormously, as can translations, themes, visual illustrations, and many other elements. Some Jews even make a point to create a new *haggadah* each year in order to keep the experience fresh.

Despite this variety, Jews often refer to the text in any version as "the *Haggadah*." Several different texts and supplements are quoted in *Rereading Exodus* with citations intended to make references as clear as possible.

Far Enough?

As we launch this journey, it is important to notice....

...Some of us reading and working with this text see ourselves as part of a Jewish or a Christian narrative in which the Exodus plays a key role. Others relate to Exodus through a political philosophy lens. Some may be coming to it as a brand new tale.

...For some of us, telling the next generation "what God did for me" (Ex 13:8) is meaningful and pertinent. For others, not so much.

Simply noticing disparate points with regard to "shared" culture is another key stage in joint efforts. Failing to do so can mean dragging each other from one *Mitzrayim* to another.

One Passover teaching, repeated and discussed for some 1500 years, says that each of us must see ourselves as personally coming forth from *Mitzrayim* (see "In Every Generation"). There are many ways of under-standing this commandment, and there is no suggestion that non-Jews are under this obligation. So, it would be a stretch to insist that we -- in this generation in the U.S. -- are obligated to re-read Exodus so as to experience coming forth from the Narrow Place of systemic racism and injustice. But we, especially white people -- in or outside Jewish communities, cannot avoid the obligation to address racism and injustice. And, in that context, we can see re-reading Exodus as a tool in that work.

The temptation is strong to believe that we've somehow come far enough already. Equally powerful, as exhibited in the Bible story itself and in our world today, is the urge to give up and return to the Narrow Place we sought to escape. It is clear, however, that we have much to learn from careful consideration of Exodus, in its long, messy, boundary-crossing complexity. And we have long known that "none of us is free if one of us is chained."

"In Every Generation"

In each and every generation,
a person must see themself
as personally coming forth from Mitzrayim.
As it is said:
"And you shall tell your child on that day, saying:
   It is because of what YHVH did for me
   when I came forth out of Mitzrayim." (Ex 13:8)

-- Mishnah Pesachim 10:5-6 [from early rabbinic writings on Passover]
   see also B. Pes 116b [Babylonian Talmud]

Midrash

The term *"Midrash"* refers to a vast array of commentary on Bible, created over the course of thousands of years and still on-going. The word comes from the Hebrew verb *derash*, "to seek out" or "interpret." Often based on close analysis of the language in a verse or comparing two or more passages, *midrash* can be narrative, sometimes called "stories about stories in the Bible," or legal.

For example, the passage above produces an action lesson from an Exodus verse. Elaborations of the text offered above by Zora Neale Hurston and Alicia Ostriker are examples of narrative or poetic *midrash*. Cassuto (below) derives interpretation from literary analysis of the text.

Other forms of commentary focus on plain sense of the text, mystical meanings, or homelitical messages.

This Millstone

What would it mean for us, collectively, to "come forth from *Mitzrayim*"? One clue is suggested by a passage, Exodus 6:1-7, in which God and Moses discuss names and big changes to come. It appears here that God intends the people to learn something new.

God says: "I appeared to Abraham, to Isaac, and to Jacob, as God Almighty [*El Shaddai*], not by My name YHVH..." (Ex 6:3). An odd thing to say, given

- YHVH was already revealed to Moses at the burning bush (Ex 3:6);

- Moses was earlier told to share the name YHVH with the children of Yisrael (Ex 3:15) and with the elders (Ex 3:18); and

- the name YHVH also appears in the first audience of Aaron and Moses with Pharaoh (Ex 5:1ff).

So, what does it mean, this "but (by) my name YHVH I was not known"? What is it that is still unknown? Umberto Cassuto (Italy, 1883–1951) argues that this unknown is a future experience.

God uses four different verbs to describe what is coming, and the People won't know God as Liberator until

> ### God's Names
>
> The four-letter name of God ("tetragrammaton") -- יהוה – is spelled yud-hey-vav-hey in Hebrew and Y-H-V-H in English. YHVH – which means something like "I will be Who I will be" -- is distinguished from other names for God, like "*El*," and "*Shaddai*" which also appear in Exodus. "The Name" is not pronounced aloud; instead, Jews often substitute "*Adonai* [Lord]" or "*HaShem* [The Name]." Many translations use "The Lord" to mean "YHVH." Some use all caps to distinguish "LORD [YHVH]" from "lord [of the property, e.g.]."

those four promises have been fulfilled....while much has been written about the four verbs, the main point here is that the People must have a series of new experiences in order to learn something new about liberation.

> ### The Four Promises
>
> The four verbs of Exodus 6:6-7 are linked to the four cups of wine at the Passover seder:
>
> (1) bring you out..."   v'hotzeiti   וְהוֹצֵאתִי
> (2) rescue you..."   v'hitzalti   וְהִצַּלְתִּי
> (3) redeem you...,"   v'gaalti   וְגָאַלְתִּי
> (4) take you*..."   v'lakachti   וְלָקַחְתִּי
>   *as a partner/spouse

"(by) my name YHVH I was not known to them.... and you shall know that I am YHVH your God, who brings you out from beneath the burdens [*sivlot*] of Egypt" -- Ex 6:3-7

We won't really know a divine Liberator, "who brings you out from beneath the burdens [*sivlot*] of *Mitzrayim*," until we collectively experience the getting out from under.

One of the things we learned in Cross River Dialogue is that shared experience, and honest discussion of separate experience, is key to our learning. Living and working near one another too seldom includes going through things together. And going through things together too seldom includes honest assessment and discussion.

Living and working near one another
too seldom includes shared experiences.
And experiencing something together too seldom includes
honest assessment and discussion.

Working through this book, alone or in a community, is one way of creat-

---

"*Sivlah*," as a noun (pl: *sivlot*), appears six times in the Torah:

Ex 1:11, discussed Stage 6;

Ex 6:6 and 6:7 discusssed here and above (Stage 5);

Ex 2:11) Moses "grows up," goes out to see his brethren, observes their "burdens [*sivlot*]," sees a *Mitzrayim-ite* strike a *Yisrael-ite* and kills the man [all in one verse, the first recorded acts of grown Moses];

Ex 5:4) Pharaoh chastises Moses and Aaron for interfering with *Yisrael-ite* work (different word: *maasav*) and tells them to get back to their own burdens [*sivlot*]; then...

Ex 5:5) rejects the request for a three-day cessation of the people's labors [*sivlot*].

The Millstone that is *Mitzrayim*

The word "*sivlot*" (plural; singular: "*sivlah*") first appears in the Exodus story when Pharaoh decides that Yisrael is becoming too big and might side with enemies.... more on this to come....

"Therefore they did set over them taskmasters to afflict them with their burdens [*sivlot*]" -- (Ex 1:11)

Referencing the expression "to afflict," Ibn Ezra (1089 - 1164 CE, Spain) suggests that the sole purpose of the labor was to inflict suffering, or, alternatively, to effectively lower the high birth-rate among *Yisrael-ites*.

Another commentary focuses on the expression "with **their** burdens," saying "their" refers to burdens or labor that had belonged to the *Mitzrayim-ites*. It seems likely this was meant straightforwardly: tasks once done by the oppressor-class was given to the oppressed to do. But the larger idea of what happens when a people or group don't shoulder their own burdens seems worth considering.

"Burden" ["*sivlah*'] in Ex 1:11 is also commonly translated as "yoke" or "oppressive work," each translation picking up on different views of *Yis-rael-ite* experience.

When Ex 6:6 -- associated with the first cup of wine at the Passover seder -- appears in *New American Haggadah* (see box), "*sivlah*" is translated with an unusual expression: "the **millstone** that is Egypt." ("Egypt" is in the original, but future quotations will use substitute the Hebrew transliteration, as discussed above and throughout this book.) Prior to 2012 I had not found "millstone" used for "burdens" in this biblical/Passover context, although the equation of racism with a millstone was common.

We are left to guess how *New American Haggadah* came to use this expression. But there is an old commentary thread (dating back to the Talmud) about Pharaoh inflicting "crushing [*b'farekh*] labor." The word *b'farekh* is an unusual in the Bible, and some ancient commentary suggests it is related to "softening," which was understood in ancient times to mean something like crushing for flour. (Image: old, worn millstone atop flour; image by Falco via Pixabay.)

Whatever path brought the translation choice for *New American Haggadah*, "the millstone that is [*Mitzrayim*]" captures the constant, grinding nature of oppression in the Exodus story, along with that of racism in the U.S. The imagery also suggests regular and fundamental alteration -- as when grain is transformed into flour -- which also seems apt for tyranny and oppression, which affects oppressor as well as oppressed.

New American Haggadah also translates the verb in Exodus 6:6 in a way that enhances the millstone metaphor: "I will lift you out from under" -- more usually translated as "bring out" or "bring out from under" -- highlights the weight involved and the difficulties in escaping it.

Exodus 6:6 appears early in the Passover Seder. At that point, we are still under the weight of old circumstances and assumptions and have not moved through the Exodus experiences meant to help us learn something new. At this point in *Rereading Exodus* we still have much to consider regarding where we are, how this millstone disproportionately affects various groups of us under it, and what it might mean to be lifted out from under.

New American Haggadah (Boston: Little Brown, 2012)
Edited by Jonathan Safran Foer. Translation by Nathan Englander.
Design by Oded Ezer. Timeline created by Mia Sara Bruch
Commentaries by
    Nathaniel Deutsch as "House of Study"
    Jeffrey Goldberg as "Nation"
    Rebecca Newberger Goldstein as "Library"
    Lemony Snicket as "Playground"

The "millstone" language is one of my favorite aspects of this *haggadah* – which, by the way, I don't recommend for use at a seder for many reasons. One of my least favorite aspects of this *haggadah* is its total lack of footnotes or source citations. My best guess at this word choice involves a passage from the Babylonian Talmud (Sotah 11b) which explores ideas of "crushing" and "soft" for the word "b'farech," used to described the labors of Exodus 1:13.

Prior to 2012, I had not seen this "millstone" wording for Exodus 6:6 in any Bible translation, other *haggadah*, or writings on this passage. I was really struck with it and searched out other examples at the time, turning up none – which is not to say they don't exist.

Aurora Levins Morales uses millstone imagery for racism, in contrast to anti-Jewish oppression which she describes with as a pressure valve, in the context of Passover as well as in this publication:

> Racism is like a millstone, a crushing weight that relentlessly presses down on people intended to be a permanent underclass. Its purpose is to press profit from us, right to the edge of extermination and beyond. The oppression of Jews is a conjuring trick, a pressure valve, a shunt that redirects the rage of working people away from the 1%, a hidden mechanism, a set up that works through misdirection, that uses privilege to hide the gears.
> -- *Understanding Antisemitism: An Offering to Our Movement*,
> A Resource from Jews for Racial & Economic Justice, 2017
> More on this publication and these ideas later.

Image: Pencil drawing, based on the previous real-life image of a millstone on flour. Top of stone reads "M-I-T-Z-R-A-Y-I-" in a circle, so first "M" of *MitzrayiM* is also the last. Hebrew word "מצרים" appears on stone's rim. Under the stone is ground flour.

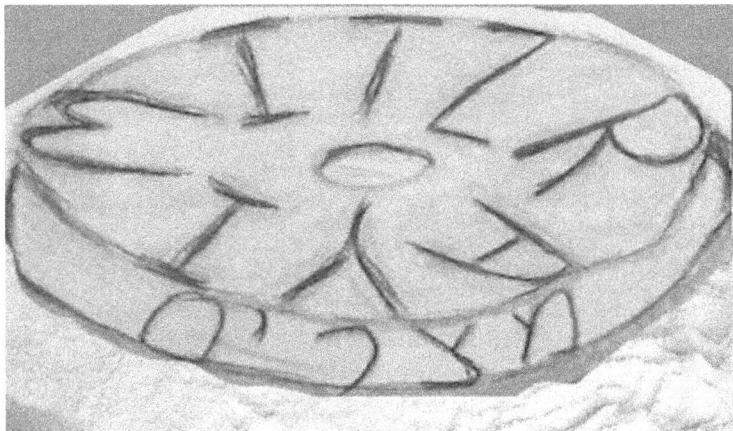

Who Are We?

One reason we re-learn the Exodus story, year after year, is to give ourselves another opportunity to grasp the many ways in which we have yet to experience Liberation. One way to seek out new perspectives is to consider ourselves as some, or all, the characters in a sacred text.

- How are we, like the midwives at the start of the story (Ex 1:15-21), attempting to stand up to power and for life?

- How are we, like Moses (Ex 2ff), struggling with identity -- raised in one household and culture but connected in many ways to another?

- How are we, like Pharaoh (Ex 1ff), impatient with the past and fearful of the future, ready to knock down anyone or anything that threatens those we believe we must protect?

- As *Yisrael-ite* or *Mitzrayim-ite*, what assumptions and experiences form our views?

Can we learn to hold more than one point of view at the same time or in conversation with one another?

Some go further and seek perspectives of non-humans in the story: the basket which carries infant Moses; The River (Nile); the bush that burns but is not consumed; the staff adult Moses carries ;the snake the staff temporarily becomes; the Sea of Reeds, before, during, or after its splitting. God.

Some people liken this method of Torah study to dream interpretation. And some teachers place this work in a therapeutic context. Please do note that, in grappling deeply with text, challenging images and memories can arise. This is one reason it's useful to work with a partner or a group.

This kind of Torah study can be the basis of additional storytelling, and other forms of artistic expression, around the sacred text. It can be used to create "Bibliodrama" with others.

The Institute for Contemporary Midrash, one of the first places I learned bibliodrama and other forms of midrashic expression, is now a web-based program, still run by its founder, Rivka Walton. Visit ICMidrash.org.

However we approach the Exodus story, one part of our learning job is to figure out how we've been contributing to the oppression of others and how we might begin to address that. It's hard work. Sometimes processing in a group can be helpful or joining in existing efforts. See "Some Resources to Explore" for a few suggestions.

Here are selections from a relevant example from Jews for Racial and Economic Justice (JFREJ). "*Maggid*" [Telling]" is the main narrative section of the Passover seder.

"After the Maggid: When We Imagine Ourselves Allies"
by Sarah Barasch-Hagans and Graie Barasch-Hagans

Author Note:
In most discussions of racial justice, interracial families are often made completely invisible. This is ironic, as these families constantly deal in a microcosm with the larger issues of white supremacy and thus have much to teach us. This piece began as a way of addressing the complexities of oppression within interracial families and pushing against how abstract and disconnected most conceptions of "allyship" can feel for white members of interracial families. The language of fighting for family may make more sense for everyone to acknowledge the experiences of an interracial family unit and of a larger multiracial human family.

...If everywhere is a desert then the sand we stand is always shifting, and so is our relationship to each other. Let us take a moment to imagine ourselves thus...

Sometimes we are Bat Pharaoh...
...Pharaoh's daughter, choosing "compassion" without hesitation, pulling the baby out of the river and giving him a home. But when we pull him from the river, he is taken from his people and forced to pretend to be someone else in order to survive. And we know that he is family and we love him as our son, but we ask impossible things of him....

Sometimes we are Moses...
...conditionally white with Cossack eyes and a quick sunburn, passing but keeping a suitcase by the door just in case. Feeling mostly safe in the palace walls, guilty but not knowing why, until one day everything changes. Until one day we see the Egyptian striking the Israelite...So sometimes we are standing next to our Black husband at the protest, and we are both chanting peacefully but the policeman strikes him and all we can do is choose not to run away, to stand firmly with our hands raised so that we both get hit. Because family means if you hit him then you hit me.

Sometimes we are Tzipporah...
...fully capable of defending ourselves but in need of a few more allies. Ready to be an ally when it means leaving our family, circumcising our children, and wandering in the desert for decades. And

some of us are still Tzipporah. Marveling at how quickly you forget this when our children are killed by the police....
-- from #*BLM Haggadah Supplement*, 2016
Download the entire publication and more from jfrej.org

The authors's note also makes the point, one that cannot be emphasized often enough: "The Exodus story is filled with allies and oppressors, with many of the characters inhabiting both roles at different points."

Considering multiple perspectives, all valid, and exploring contradictory realities, all true, is key in collaboration and community building. It is also a traditional way to read Jewish sacred text. This can be confusing for people not used to this way of reading, especially this approach to Bible -- which some of us were taught had "the meaning" we needed a particular sort of teacher to impart.

The Peoples' Companion to the Bible, cited above, explains this neatly, using the example of Fortress Press' own "commentary from the respected Hermeneia series" for comparison:

> While the Hermeneia commentary page is designed to focus attention on the most accurate determination of "the meaning" of the text that a single scholar can provide, the Rabbinic Bible is designed to draw on a *variety* of voices interpreting a single text.
> -- p. xxvii, Introduction, *The Peoples' Companion to the Bible*

Throughout *Rereading Exodus,* we will see that Bible passages yield readings focused on individuals and interpersonal relationships, on systemic racism, on anti-Jewishness, on the intersection of those and other forms of oppression, and on many other facets of the text. All those layers are contained within the text. Even if we're discussing which one adheres more closely to the grammar at one point or some other element of the text, or which makes more sense in one particular context, all the layers are there.

That variety is an important tool. And, as with any tool, taking care in its use is essential.

[ritual questions are out of order here; sorry!
For Passover-related reasons, "we counted 6" is
linked with "Roundabout and Old Bones" below]

"The Exodus story is filled with allies and oppressors, with many of the characters inhabiting both roles at different points."
-- from #*BLM Haggadah Supplement*, 2016

----------------Some Resources to Explore----------------

Ammud provides Jewish education for Jews of Color, by Jews of Color. Many of their programs are accessible on-line now. As a white Jew, I have not participated directly in Ammud's regular programs, but I have been inspired when their teachers present in the wider world. They also offer an opportunity to stay in touch through their "Ally Circle." Ammud.org

Drisha was one of the, if not *the*, earliest places for women to learn advanced classical text. Their offerings have expanded to wider adult Jewish education, and much is now available on-line, including many useful approaches to Exodus. I have learned with Drisha in-person and on-line and highly recommend for the more text-focused among us. Drisha.org

Jews for Racial and Economic Justice is based in New York and focuses on local issues but also provides materials, including *#BLM Haggadah Supplement* and other materials of wide use plus programming that supports understanding Jewish text and ritual in a social justice context. jfrej.org/

Jews in ALL Hues (JIAH) is an education and advocacy organization supporting Jews of Color and multi-heritage Jews. They aim "to build a future for the Jewish people where intersectional diversity and dignity are normative." Workshops include "Practical Allyship and Liberation," and "The Intersection of Racism, Judaism, and White Supremacy." jewsinallhues.org/

SVARA: The Traditionally Radical Yeshiva focuses on Talmud, rather than Bible, and might appear at first glance too advanced or too heavy and maybe too far removed from Exodus. But SVARA is dedicated in everything it does to promoting racial justice and examining oppression and privilege, thereby offering new angles on Exodus themes. They call their style "hardcore, queer, and radically inclusive," and are the most supportive, soul-affirming learning of any kind I've met yet. There are free opportunities to try out their learning and all classes are pay-what-you-can. svara.org

Tzedek Chicago is "an intentional Jewish congregation based on core values of justice, equity and solidarity." Torah study, which has been on-line since early in the pandemic, is open to all and draws people from around the world and from many backgrounds. Rabbi Brant Rosen strives to make discussion accessible. The weekly studies are focused on portion of the week, so not necessarily about Exodus all the time; however, issues of equity and community building are constant themes. tzedekchicago.org

Uri L'Tzedek is an orthodox Jewish social justice organization. Their resources include Torah teachings in text, webinars, and other resources of use in anti-racism and other Exodus-related work. utzedek.org

----

Who Are We Not?

Exodus opens with that list of names discussed above, Jacob/*Yisrael* and his eleven sons. The text then adds:

> Joseph was in Egypt already. -- Ex 1:5

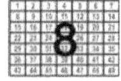

Joseph is mentioned twice more in the next few verses and then again in Ex 13:9. His role in this saga is pivotal, and -- aware that where we begin is crucial to a story's shape -- knowing a little about Joseph will be important in *Rereading Exodus*.

In his 1974 *Bible Tales with Commentary*, Dick Gregory (*z"l*) provides a summary, excerpted here ("From The ABC's of Slavery"), before he launches his commentary, which is insightful on its own and useful for our purposes, simultaneously dated and way too current.

Gregory begins his commentary with notes on dreamers and dreaming:

> Joseph found out it's dangerous to be a dreamer. Just like Joseph's brothers, society today has three ways of dealing with dreamers. Kill the dreamer. Throw the dreamer in jail (the contemporary "cisterns" in our society). Or sell the dreamer into slavery; purchase the dream with foundation grants or government deals, until the dreamer becomes enslaved to controlling financial or governmental interests. Society tries to buy off the dream and lull the dreamer to sleep. It's called a "lull-a-buy." -- *Bible Tales*, p.70

In this 1974 publication, Gregory goes on to say that Dr. Martin Luther King, Jr. "experienced all the ways society tries to deal with dreamers," concluding: "Dreamers can be killed. Dreams live on."

Today, as in 1974, readers of many backgrounds can relate to a system that tries to destroy dreams by attacking dreamers.

It is noteworthy in Gregory's presentation here that MLK is introduced without explicit reference to race; in contrast to elsewhere in the same book, where King's Blackness is highlighted, this passage portrays the leader more generally as a dreamer who treaded in dangerous political territory.

Gregory then shifts to a more racially explicit perspective, suggesting that "maybe Joseph was a Black cat." He continues, regarding Joseph's incarceration and interpretation of dreams for fellow inmates (Gen 40):

> The butler in the Joseph story symbolizes America's treatment of Black folks. The butler used Joseph's talent as an interpreter of dreams and he promised to tell Pharaoh about Joseph. As soon as

the butler got himself comfortably back in Pharaoh's palace, he forgot about his word to Joseph.

America was built on the sweat, toil, and talent of Black folks. But when the work was done and the talent utilized, America quickly forgot its debt to Blacks. Black folks helped lay down the railroad tracks, but they could only work as porters after the trains started running. Black slaves picked the cotton, but the garment industry belonged to white folks. -- *Bible Tales*, p.73

Then, as now, readers outside Black communities can relate to the feeling of being ill-used. But here Gregory specifically references the experience of Black people enslaved in the U.S. and their descendants. Those of us for whom this is not direct experience must recognize what we know and what we don't know.

We might consider the dreamer passage **outside-in**, bringing outside experience to illuminate sacred text, while the butler passage works **inside-out**, bringing sacred text to illuminate the outside world. These forms of Torah overlap, and we can all learn from both. It is crucial for all of us to listen to and try to empathize with views not our own. But these two forms of commentary from Dick Gregory illustrate crucial reminders for Passover and year-round:

- Each generation must see ourselves as though we actually left *Mitzrayim*, but that experience alone does not make us first-hand experts on topics like "America's treatment of Black folks."

- We must carefully distinguish between learning about others' experiences, on the one hand, and mistaking it for our own, on the other.

Dick Gregory (1932-2017, *z"l*) was an author, comedian, civil rights leader, health educator, activist, and mentor. Among his writings, *Dick Gregory's Bible Tales with Commentary* (James R. McGraw, ed. NY: Stein and Day, 1974) is an often neglected treasure.

Gregory was long active in school desegregation and other efforts in Chicago and ran for mayor in 1967. He was later active for decades in the DC area. He was mentor to many, including members of CRD. Gregory supported Kymone Freeman's organizing of Black LuvFest, for example, and founding of We Act Radio, where he was interviewed at length. His six-hour funeral, in Landover, MD, included celebrity tributes, remarks from local and national government figures as well as just a tiny number of the people whose lives he touched.

From "The ABC's of Slavery,"

Dick Gregory's Bible Tales with Commentary James R. McGraw, ed.
NY: Stein and Day, 1974 (Harper & Row/Perennial Paperback also 1974)

"A. Dealing with the Dreamer (Genesis Chapter 37)"

Joseph was one of many brothers and half-brothers. But because Joseph had been born in Jacob's old age, he was the favorite of his father. Jacob was always doing things for Joseph, dressing him up in boss threads and fine vines [1974, remember]. For example, he gave Joseph a long-sleeved coat of many different colors, a style that was really in at the time. [p.63]

Joseph's brothers couldn't stand him. They thought he was a spoiled brat, a tattletale, and Daddy's little pet. Of course, Joseph brought much of the hatred on himself. For example, he just couldn't resist telling his dreams to his brothers....

So they sold Joseph for 20 shekels and the traders took Joseph to Egypt....

...The traders sold Joseph to Potiphar, the captain of Pharaoh's guard. The dreamer was about to start a new career in the court of Pharaoh. But that's another story. [pp.64-65. See also **"B. The Butler, the Baker and the Captain's Wife** (Genesis Chapters 39-40)" not excerpted here.]

"C. Feast and Famine (Genesis Chapter 41)"

...And Joseph was given the second chariot behind Pharaoh, and wherever he rode, people got down on their knees before him. So Joseph did his Charlton Heston bit throughout the land of Egypt.

And Joseph put his conservation program into effect. In every city food from the surrounding fields was stored up....

Then the famine came. There was no food in all the earth, except in the land of Egypt. The people cried out in their hunger to Pharaoh, and Pharaoh said, "Go see Joseph and do whatever he says."...

And Joseph said to Pharaoh one day, "Good business just requires patience. I knew we'd get a good wheat deal if we had sense enough to wait seven years." [p.70. end of Gregory's summary; end of excerpt]

Two additional notes about the biblical Joseph:
1) He is great-grandson of Sarah and Abraham; grandson of Rebecca and Isaac; and son of Rachel and Jacob/*Yisrael*.
2) As Genesis ends, he arranges for his extended family to settle in *Mitzrayim*, and as Exodus opens, that clan of 70 re-appears.

Photos: Left and below: two book covers for *Dick Gregory's Bible Tales*, both 1974
Right: Dick Gregory at Black LuvFest 2017.

Top left: Trade paperback cover, with title, "Dick Gregory's Bible Tales with Commentary" in slight arc over photo of dark-haired Dick Gregory, smiling slightly, dressed in costume of biblical-looking robe with scroll in his left hand. Below left: Mass market paperback cover with title superimposed on image of Gregory, posing as Moses atop a mountain with two stone tablets in arm.

Right: Silver-haired Gregory (looking, at 85, very like his picture at 42, excepting the gray hair) in tan summer suit, tie, and light-colored shirt, squinting into the sun, alone in front of a small crowd interacting among display stalls; between Gregory and the festival are two large cement planters filled with bedraggled plants.

NOTE: *Dick Gregory's Bible Tales with Commentary* was written a long time ago. Parts of it are outdated in cute, nostalgic ways, like the reference to how we'd only have three commandments if Rose Mary Woods had been in charge.... Duck-Duck-Go it if need be (or use a search engine that tracks your movements and sells them to marketers, if that's your preference).... Parts of it show its age in ways in that just remind us how long ago the 1970s are. But it still has power, some of which comes from the fact that it was written so long ago, and some of which comes from Gregory's perception and wit. However, the book has been out of print for decades. Stein and Day are long gone. I am looking into possibilities for having it re-published and would love to hear from anyone with thoughts on this.

Roundabout and Old Bones

The previous section took us back to the Joseph story in Genesis, an essential precursor leading to the Exodus story. Here, we continue to orient ourselves for the journey, with a jump ahead: past 13 chapters of drama, to what is sometimes understood as "the Exodus," the point when the *Yisrael-ites* finally leave *Mitzrayim* and then cross the Sea of Reeds.

Getting out is a goal for the first 13 chapters of Exodus and then a climax in the story. The triumphant moment appears in the Torah portion called "*Beshalach*" (Exodus 13:17-17:16), including the Song of the Sea sung by grateful *Yisrael-ites* after they escape Pharaoh's army...

....In *The Prince of Egypt*, I'm told, the Song occurs before they get through the sea; not sure if/how that changes experience of the moment -- worth considering for those for whom that movie is part of their vision here....

The triumphant moment of the Exodus -- the fact that it's always at least one of the end-points for this drama -- sometimes overshadows the complexities of the story. This can fool us into thinking we're freer than we are. It can also hinder us from noticing some useful things

The Song of the Sea has long been part of Jewish liturgy, as have psalms that celebrate coming out of *Mitzrayim* (Psalms 113-118, "Egyptian Hallel"). Celebratory Exodus themes are part of many other moments in the daily, Shabbat and Festival prayers, as well as Passover. But these triumphal elements have also long raised conflict.

Jewish tradition has always included the bitter along with the sweet and asked us to recognize painful parts of the Exodus story – for example, the ritual removing of wine from our Passover cup for each of the ten plagues. For many Jews, however, this is not enough. See, e.g., *Siddur Dvar Hadash* and "Red Sea," quoted in the Introduction. But change leads through conflict...

about the text. The portion "*Beshalach*" (see box) opens with noteworthy complexities.   [Again, ritual questions are out of order here; sorry!]

Change of Heart, Old Promises

First, the *Yisrael-ites* are sent on a roundabout route, to avoid a "change of heart." Seeking to avoid war is a worthy motive. But the text here suggests that the People are being sent on a roundabout way because they might fear conflict: The verb translated as "change of heart" [nachum, נחם] also means "comfort." So, there is a strong sense that this particular leadership decision is about seeking comfort over facing even potential conflict (Ex 13:17-18 -- see box).

from *Beshalach*

When Pharaoh sent the people out,
God did not lead them [*v'lo-nacham*]
by the coastal/Philistine route, although it was nearer, for God said:
"Lest the people may have a change of heart [*pen yinnachem*]
when they see war, and return to Egypt."
So God led the people roundabout, by wilderness route,
at the Sea of Reeds...
And Moses took the bones of Joseph with him;
for he had extracted a vow from the Children of *Yisrael*, saying:
"God will surely remember you;
and you shall carry up my bones away with you."
-- Exodus 13:17-19

Then we're told that the *Yisrael-ites* are carting along old bones. This is to honor a vow made generations earlier, back when the old Pharaoh still knew Joseph (Gen 50:24-26 and Ex 1:8, Ex 13:19).

In regard to this promise, there are commentaries from many perspectives. Some of the most ancient look at ritual concerns; while beyond the scope of this book, it is worth noting that questions around respectful treatment of the dead are age-old concerns from many traditions.

R' Nachman of Breslov (1772-1810 CE, Ukraine) teaches that carrying Joseph's bones can be understood as Moses, "the aspect of the mind," being bound to Joseph "the aspect of the *tzaddik* [untranslated in Breslov Institute's English]." Although *tzaddik* can be translated as "virtuous" or "just," it also means "to be clear." So, carrying Joseph's bones is binding clarity to mind. (*Likutei Moharan.* 211:1)

One symbolic approach links Joseph with a quality the *Yisrael-ites* need for this trip. R' Nachman (see left) has a specific quality in mind. But, as we learn more about the biblical Joseph, we can also ponder if/how he exemplifies a quality the People need here and what that quality might be.

Sforno (16th Century, Italy; see above) again offers us political practicalities:

> ...any obligation undertaken communally must be honoured by the leader of that community when the time and opportunity presents itself to discharge that obligation (Eliyahu Munk trans. via Sefaria).

This raises many questions, including: What does it mean for a community to be obligated? How does that come about, and how is it discharged? What do we owe leaders, or other community members, of the past?

Liberation and Conflict

Finally, as if to underscore the illusory nature of liberation, the *Yisrael-ites* are sent out of the Narrow Place and meant to believe escape is at hand. But, they are again trapped, with *Mitzrayim*'s army behind and the Sea of Reeds ahead (Ex 14; not quoted here).

The Bible story continues with God helping Moses to part the waters, the escaping People marching "into the sea on dry ground," the sea "coming back upon" the pursuing chariots and riders, and, finally, the *Yisrael-ites* emerging on the other side with Pharaoh no longer a threat.

Hurston describes events this way:

> "Well, he's got the great big sea over him, and I reckon that's big enough to suit anybody."
>
> They made a song on that and danced it off. A man with a good voice got out in the center of the ring and sang.
>
> "Old Pharaoh's dead!"
>
> And the chorus answered, "How did he die?"
>
> And the solo man went to dancing and said: "Well, he died like this!" and he dance that off. Then he sang another part and every-body went on dancing and shouting.
>
> "Oh, he died in his chariot and he died in the sea And he wouldn't have died at all if he let us be."
>
> They sang that over and over and danced on it until they got tired. Then Miriam took the cymbal and some more women went behind her and they went all over the camp singing...
> -- Hurston, *Moses*, p.193-194 (see also Exodus 15:1-20)

The Exodus story itself is calling us to consider how we deal with conflict and the fear of it:

How often have those not actively suffering from oppression been the ones to decide what the times will bear?

How many times, over how many centuries, have those seeking justice heard, from in their own communities and beyond --

> "Now is not the time..."
> "You're too young to know" and/or "You're too old to understand."
> "Be patient. That's what works in the end."
> "You'll get us all killed."
> "We are better off with the devil we know."

Have we learned more about approaching conflict that to help us this time?

And what about these old bones?

Are we honoring ancestors by carrying them?
Or are we tied to older visions and promises that are holding us back,
might even shame those same ancestors?

What does it mean for a community to be obligated?
How does that come about, and how is it discharged?
What do we owe leaders,
or other community members, of the past?

Charnice Milton Community Book

Gift Cards   Best Sellers   New Releases   Fiction   Nonfiction   YA   Kids   En Español   Games & Puzzles

$19,828,627.33 raised for local bookstores

Charnice Milton Community Bookstore

Booklists on CMCB's Bookshop include

Jewish Virtual Bookstore:
Filling a Gap, Supporting Community
For DC area Jews and others who lack a convenient, inclusive resource

Women Named on DC Buildings
Women we should know, named on schools and other buildings/operations in the nation's capital

We Act Radio Authors

America's Islamic Heritage Museum Recommends

Abolition and Related Topics

Race, Color, Jews, Bible, and Identity

For Young Readers from Our Themed Lists

30% of all purchases go directly to local literacy programs and book distribution.

Communities and Obligations

Chapter 1 began, as the Book of Exodus does, with one group of people moving into an area that is new to them. We looked at a variety of perspectives and tools for exploring relationships between two cultural groups, now sharing the same land. This chapter looks more closely at possibilities and challenges of cross-cultural living: in *Mitzrayim*, in DC, and in our wider world today.

In particular, this chapter more fully introduces DC's Cross River Dialogue and explores the impact of personal relationships and intergroup dialogue on the polity as a whole -- again using groups inside DC to understand *Mitzrayim* and vice versa.

As for progress through the Book of Exodus itself: Previously, we jumped briefly ahead to conversations between God and Moses (Ex Chapter 6) and to crossing of the Sea of Reeds (Ex Chapters 13- 15) -- so we know there's an escape ahead. We also jumped back to some of Joseph's story (Gen Chapters 37, 39-50), as part of our mapping the landscape.

Early in this chapter, we jump ahead again to preparation for departure and consideration of who does, and does not, leave the Narrow Place.

In many ways, though, we are still at the beginning of the tale:

> Now these are the names of the sons of *Yisrael,* who came into
> *Mitzrayim* with Jacob...and Joseph was in *Mitzrayim* already.
> And Joseph died, and all his brethren, and all that generation.
> And the children of Israel were fruitful...and filled the land
> Now there arose a new king over *Mitzrayim*, who did not know
> Joseph. And he said unto his people: 'Behold, the people of the
> children of *Yisrael* are too many and too mighty for us...'
> Therefore they set taskmasters to afflict them with their burdens.
> And they built for Pharaoh store-cities, Pithom and Ramses...
> And the *Mitzrayim-ites* made the *Yisrael-ites* serve with crushing
> labor. And they made their lives bitter with hard service...
> -- from Exodus 1:1-14

Scattered within *Mitzrayim*

Exodus text tells us very little about interaction between ordinary *Yisrael-ites* and *Mitzrayim-ites*. It is not even clear where the two groups lived, relative to one another. Commentary to address these unknowns is vast and varied, reflecting a range of Jewish views on cross-cultural experiences.

R' Benno Jacob, for example, argues, based on clues in the narrative itself:

> The details of our story suggest that [the *Yisrael-ites*] were scattered throughout [*Mitzrayim*], which must have led to many personal friendships; only a systematically encouraged hate propaganda was able to change this. -- B. Jacob, *The Second Book of the Bible* p.343

This viewpoint may seem unremarkable, if a little preachy...until considering that it comes from a rabbi living in Germany during the Third Reich. Watching synagogues burn and community members shipped off to concentration camps, he continued to indict "a systematically encouraged hate propaganda," rather than the neighbors. This perspective strongly affirms the humanity in those many would see as enemies. It also raises questions about personal friendships amidst "a systematically encouraged hate propaganda."

Rabbi Benno Jacob (1862-1945) was born in Breslau and active in German Jewish life through the 1930s. He was still in Germany when most synagogues were burned. He saw the German Jewish community to which he'd dedicated his life destroyed and witnessed the deportation to Dachau (and later return) of his son, R' Ernst Jacob.

Benno Jacob lost nearly everything in moving to England in his late seventies. There he spent his last five years, completing his Exodus commentary in 1940, continuing to revise until his death, at 83, in 1945.

A few years ago, R' Shai Held of Mechon Hadar communicated with Benno Jacob's son to confirm that the author was working on this Exodus commentary between 1934 and 1939, while still in Germany.

If the propaganda succeeded while individuals from two groups were living side-by-side, would the effect be more or less pronounced for groups physically separately or otherwise insulated from one another?

If existing personal friendships were, in fact, changed through propaganda, might they have instead survived with additional support?

Can personal friendships ameliorate the effects of systematic oppression? Help dismantle it?

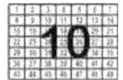

These and similar questions run through the development of intergroup dialogue, like the one formed in DC in 2018, across the Anacostia River.

Not So Scattered

In early 2018, a DC official and community leader posted an off-the-cuff remark on Facebook Live that was picked up by local, national, and international news outlets. The brief video set off a firestorm of controversy that eventually touched the Nation of Islam, locally and nationally, Jews near and far, and many other elements in electoral and community politics. It has yet to entirely dissipate, and its embers are regularly fanned.

...The contents of the original message, and what happened to the City program that provoked them are a fascinating story for another forum....

What's most important in the context of Exodus and R' Jacob's thought about friendship and propaganda is that the loudest voices were completely isolated from one another in daily life. R' Jacob suggested that personal friendships must have developed between *Yisrael-ites* and *Mitzrayim-ites* because *Yisrael-ite* residences were scattered throughout *Mitzrayim*. As the controversy in DC grew, however, it became apparent that many people in predominantly Black east of the river areas had simply never met a Jew or never had a real conversation about Jewish life or Judaism with a Jew. It also became apparent that many white Jews had never been east of the river or interacted with residents of the area on their own turf.

Several times in this period someone I'd known for years through work east of the river suddenly noticed the *kippah* [head covering called "*yarmulke*" in Yiddish] I'd worn all along and said: "Hey, you're a Jew right? So, tell me..." Curiosity, not animosity or vitriol came my way from Black non-Jews.

In that same period, some white Jews did seek me out with curiosity in mind. Sadly, however, many more times than I could count, white Jews west of the river shared extreme vitriol about an individual and whole community they didn't know. Even Jews who regularly engage in peace-building and related efforts appeared to me -- again, in my own personal experiences and interpretation of them -- cavalier about promoting, intentionally or not, aspersions toward a whole population, without regard for the damage.

Some of us, in our overlapping Black and Jewish communities, worried that heavy-duty systematic encouragement of hate propaganda was underway in more than one direction. The situation was disturbing on many levels and impacting the election season. Kymone Freeman, co-owner of We Act Radio, a Black non-Jew, and I, then a regular broadcaster on the station, talked about possible responses. We recorded a few short essays and together joined a program on the topic at our sister radio station, WPFW. Together with WPFW's "To Heal DC" program -- co-hosted for decades by Chuck Hicks and Joni Eisenberg -- we decided to host a party on election night, which happened to be Juneteenth, in an effort to build some bridges.

Division and Bridge

While it did not draw a huge crowd, the party did foster some connections, including the precursor meeting for Cross River Dialogue.

Sig Cohen, a white Jew who had been working in a number of volunteer positions that brought him back and forth across the river, shared at the party that he had been considering some kind of dialogue group to address our city's divides. Not long afterward, Sig brought together five of us from that party and seven more, Jewish and not, from east and west of the river, to meet and discuss possibilities for Dialogue.

The group's history illustrates some of the possibilities and limitations of "Dialogue" and the role of personal relationships in addressing wider cultural and political divides.

June 2018 flyer for Juneteenth Building Bridges Watch Party.

Background graphic is We Act Radio storefront.

Flyer text reads: "After an election season that included strife and misunderstandings between Jewish and black communities, plus so many other difficult challenges for our neighborhoods and city as a whole...We Act Radio, WPFW's "To Heal DC" & other partners invite you to Juneteenth Building Bridges Election Watch Party."

The Anacostia River has long divided east and west in DC, helped maintain most persistent demographic and privilege divides, and evolved into a symbol for what separates us in the District. Jews live and work on both sides of this divide. All DC's formal Jewish communities and institutions and most Jewish residences, however, have long been west of the river.

The Cross River Dialogue was formed to help address the divide -- and the role of Jews in both preserving it and attempting to break it down. CRD began as a small group of white Jews living west of the Anacostia River and Black non-Jews living and/or working east of the River. It took some time for CRD to agree on that description of our group, and the process forced us to consider how we identify ourselves and others, and how a group identity can serve to both reveal and hide.

No two of our six Jews came from the same background, and together brought connections to several movements within Judaism and substantial differences of belief and practice, or lack thereof; we disagreed at first about identifying ourselves as "white." (More on Jews as "white" to come.)

No two of our five non-Jews came from the same background, and together brought connections to several strands of Christianity as well as other spiritualities and lack thereof; all identify as "Black," although some use the term "Black American" and some do not.

Image: River and bridge viewed from Anacostia Park (east looking west), perspective is level of river, looking at supports and underside of bridge up toward traffic level and directional signs.

Beyond those few identities, our group spanned differences in class, wealth, family structure, education, and political affiliation. CRD barely scratched the surface in terms of understanding what divides and what unites us.

East of the Anacostia river has long housed DC's highest proportions of poverty, illiteracy, crime and violence, amid the fewest grocery stores and medical facilities; west of the river includes far stronger infrastructure overall and pockets of privilege in terms of education, wealth, and crime rates. The population east of the river is, and has long been, predominantly Black and mostly non-Jewish while most Jews and every predominantly white neighborhood are west of the Anacostia.

Every DC Jewish school, congregation, JCC, etc. is west of the River, most located far northwest. Jewish cemeteries east of the river were founded by congregations west of the river. Only in the last few years has the city's eastern-most congregation, Hill Havurah, grown enough to sustain stable office and worship space and hire a rabbi. Another congregation, "New Synagogue Project," several years old now, is located in a neighborhood neither predominantly white nor far Northwest.

Common and Disparate

One of the tools CRD used in furthering dialogue was the Exodus story. We explored its themes early on and gathered for a special seder on the eighth night of Passover in 2019.

CRD's makeshift *haggadah* included materials borrowed from a variety of sources and a few words of our own. We opted for primarily Jewish, rather than multi-faith or universalist, sources.

In preparing, Jewish participants had the usual disagreements about what is essential in a seder in terms of text and food, ideal length and inclusion of Hebrew, which tunes are "traditional," and -- most relevant for this discussion -- what constitutes the "spiritual" and the "political."

We began our seder:

> Freedom and slavery, liberation and oppression, are both always present and always possible. We arrive at the Passover table strong and grateful for one another; for our ever-growing movement for justice and liberation.
>
> In the words of the poet and activist, Aurora Levins Morales: "This time we cannot cross until we carry each other....This time it's all of us or none."
>
> We come together on this Eighth Night of Passover, understood in Midrash, the tales about the tales in the Bible, to be the point at which we are poised on the edge of the Sea of Reeds, with Pharaoh's army at our backs -- between a series of terrible plagues behind us and an unknown future ahead.
> -- *CRD Haggadah* (not published)

We closed with impromptu singing of Bob Marley's "Redemption Song," reminding us of commonalities and differences around the table:

> Old pirates, yes, they rob I
> Sold I to the merchant ships
> Minutes after they took I
> From the bottomless pit...
>
> Won't you help to sing
> These songs of freedom?
> 'Cause all I ever have
> Redemption songs, Redemption songs
>
> Emancipate yourselves from mental slavery
> None but ourselves can free our minds...
> -- Bob Marley, 1980

On the one hand, we can all join in songs of freedom and work to emancipate ourselves from mental slavery; on the other hand, not everyone at that table shares a family background of being sold to the merchant ships, or the same relationship to Marcus Garvey's philosophy. Acknowledging both elements -- the common and the disparate -- in our experiences is crucial.

Aurora Levins Morales is "a writer, an artist, a historian, a teacher and mentor...also an activist, a healer, a revolutionary." Her "Red Sea," has been included on a variety of platforms and publications, including the JVP [Jewish Voice for Peace] Metro DC Haggadah (2019):

> ...This time that country
> is what we promise each other,
> our rage pressed cheek to cheek until tears
> flood the space between,
> until there are no enemies left,
> because this time no one will be left to drown
> and all of us must be chosen.
> This time it's all of us or none.

Her *Rimonim* [Pomegranate] Liturgy Project works with Jews in different communities to craft new liturgy that reflects, among other goals: a full integration of the lives and experiences of Indigenous Jews and Jews of Color of all backgrounds; and a deep commitment to fundamental social transformation in keeping with our deeply held principles of justice.

The full poem "Red Sea" is available, along with much more, at the author's website. www.auroralevinsmorales.com/red-sea.html

No Monolith

Acknowledging the common and the disparate in our experiences is, as just discussed, crucial. This requires care to avoid focusing on labels and pigeonholing ourselves and others.

R' Gerry Serotta (Contemporary U.S.) stresses that it is a mistake to consider either *Mitzrayim* or *Yisrael* in the Exodus story as monolithic. Here are some thoughts on the two peoples that I learned from Rabbi Gerry, who has spent decades in interfaith, pluralistic, and boundary-crossing work.

Yisrael-ites: As briefly noted above, commentary describes quite a variety of possible relationships between *Yisrael-ites* and *Mitzrayim-ites*. We'll keep raising some of these as *Rereading Exodus* continues.

Moreover, there is an old (dating from 2nd Century CE) teaching that only one in five among the people of *Yisrael* left *Mitzrayim*, while 80% -- "unworthy," or those who chose not to leave -- died in the plague of darkness (jumping ahead to Ex 10:20ff).

One in Five

Another explanation of *'chamushim'* (in Ex 13:18) [usually: 'armed'] is: only one out of five [c*hamishah*] went forth from Egypt, and four parts of the people died during the three days of darkness because they were unworthy of being delivered." – Rashi (France, 1040-1105) based on *Mekhilta d'Rabbi Yishmael* (Palestine, c. 135 CE)

Mitzrayim-ites: *Shemot Rabbah* (compilation of older commentaries, probably collected around 1200 CE) describes three groups of *Mitzrayim-ites*:

- those who left with the Israelites, "and also the *erev-rav*" -- often "mixed multitudes"; Robert Alter translates this as "motley throng" (Ex 12:38; related to "*asaf suf*" in Numbers 11:4; more later);

- those who revolted against Pharaoh and gave provisions (Ex 12:35); and

- Pharaoh, with any other unrepentant oppressors.

With only one-fifth of the *Yisrael-ites* leaving and some portion of the *Mitzrayim-ites* joining them, the People who go through the Sea of Reeds might be more of a self-selected group than we often suppose.

A Different Lens

We should not assume, Rabbi Gerry insists, that some demographic element -- ethnicity, class, etc. -- defined membership in the group that eventually leaves *Mitzrayim* to become the desert-wandering People *Yisrael*. Instead, he wants readers of Exodus to ask:

> What was it that compelled some people to leave the Narrow Place and seek liberation outside of the circumstances they previously knew? And how can we emulate THAT?

In addition, Rabbi Gerry says, we see, from early on in the Bible, that "variety is God's plan." For example, the Tower of Babel story shows God objecting when the people settle in one place, becoming "of one language" or, "one idea" (Genesis 11). This theme of God preferring variety continues in the Bible and is seen in Jewish exile and dispersion.

All this means that it is good practice to look for the variety of people and perspectives in biblical narrative.

Judaism's idea that God prefers variety may seem contrary to a tale repeating "You are MY people and I am YOUR God" and "Let My people go that they may serve ME." Variety is found in the Exodus tale, however, and in centuries of Jewish teaching centered around it.

Seeking out and naming variety within biblical stories helps us avoid pigeonholing people and stereo-typing groups in the text, in history, and in contemporary life. Exploring and amplifying difference-celebrating strands of Jewish teaching, from ancient times to the present, provides a foundation for intergroup understanding and cooperation.

What was it that compelled some people to leave behind the Narrow Place and seek liberation outside of the circumstances they previously knew? And how can we emulate THAT?

It can also be useful to seek out and name variety and commonalities within historical experience. The *CRD Haggadah* included (see next page) a Maggid section developed for a seder table with people of Irish ancestry, among others.

From the CRD Haggadah

Originally Spatz/O'Brien Family Haggadah, sources cited are as follows:

RH = Russell, Thaddeus. *A Renegade History of the United States.*
RJ = powell, john a. *Racing to Justice*
IBW = Ignatiev, Noel. *How the Irish Became White.*
Whiteness = Harris, Cheryl I. "Whiteness as Property"
(full citations in Bibliography)

When you get there, bring your fruits, call out and say: "My ancestor was a wandering Aramean.

> *Yisrael* descended to *Mitzrayim* and resided there in small numbers. He became a nation, great, powerful, and numerous. Then the *Mitzrayim-ites* treated us badly...We cried out...God heard our voice...and took us out of *Mitzrayim*." (Deut 26:5-8)

From a variety of shores, by various means, we arrived in what became the US. Our ancestors – whenever arriving willingly or not – joined a colonial system that categorized residents by race, advantaged persons identified as "White," promoted segregation, and forbade intermarriage. They were part of a European settlement that used force and law to separate indigenous people from their land and their culture. Until very recently, laws across our nation punished homosexual behavior and supported only heterosexual marriages. The system gave many rights only to men. It supported subjugation, and sometimes persecution, of many people who appeared different in some way.

From its earliest days, our nation restricted citizenship to free White people, later explicitly excluding Asians and Hispanics. Immigration policies were intertwined with views on "whiteness." Legal decisions in our country held that race was defined by popular perception and that a "reputation of whiteness" was a form of property to which only some people were entitled.

"For many being white automatically ensured higher economic returns in the short term as well as greater economic, political, and social security in the long run. Being white meant gaining access to a set of public and private privileges that materially and permanently guaranteed basic needs and survival. Being white increased the possibility of controlling critical aspects of one's life rather than of being the object of another's domination." (**RJ**)

Whiteness was "jealously guarded as a valued possession, allowed only to those who met a strict standard of proof" (**Whiteness**). New immigrants entering this system, however unwittingly, fought to prove their whiteness in order to achieve the benefits of citizenship.

Irish immigrants, arriving in large numbers in the early 19th Century, were consider non-white or, in some common parlance, "white niggers." Irish people were linked in popular press with hard drinking, brawling, unsuitability for work, and "wild dancing." White skin made the Irish "eligible for membership in the white race, [but] it did not guarantee their admission; they had to earn it." (**IBW**)

Irish America leaders engaged in concerted efforts to change perceptions. One battlefield was culture, with "ballads, including...'When Irish Eyes Are Smiling,' which came to symbolize the sober, romantic, chaste, and nondancing Irish who were invented to replace the white simians of old." By the early 20th Century, European categories, used in U.S. public policy for most of the century, included Irish among the superior "Nordic" division (**RH**).

Jews arriving before the U.S. Civil War included slaveowners and -traders as well as abolitionists. Over the decades, popular belief and U.S. public policy rendered Jews as dangerous outsiders, limiting Jewish immigration and access to social and economic life. During the same periods, popular perception treated Jews as unduly influential in economic and political spheres. Jews were portrayed as responsible for both radical leftist politics to the U.S. and for the evils of capitalism. Into the 20th Century, public schools in Philadelphia required students to note their racial identity and did not allow Jews to identify as American.

The Leo Frank rape case (1915), resulting in Frank's lynching, is just one example of popular perception painting Jews and Negroes alike as hyper-sexual, primitive, indulgent people outside "whiteness."

When Booker T. Washington compared lynchings of U.S. blacks with pogroms against Russian Jews, several Jewish papers objected to the parallel, attacking the morals of Negroes in the process. "Many Jewish leaders not only rejected such racist attacks but also committed much of their lives to the cause of black civil rights. Yet many such leaders were guided by a belief in Jewish cultural superiority and a paternalistic impulse to help the unevolved." (**RH**)

"Like the first Irish immigrants, eastern European Jews who settled in the United States seemed unaware of or unconcerned with the American color line." (**RH**).

Black, Jewish and Irish histories entwined in the U.S., producing tap dance and stepping, minstrel shows and the Gershwins, syncretism and antagonism, and, along the way, some quintessentially "American" culture.

"The outraged white citizen had been sincere when he snatched the whips from the Southern sheriffs...[But] White Americans left the Negro on the ground and in devastating numbers walked off with the aggressor," Martin Luther King, Jr. wrote in 1967. What has changed since then?

"God brought us to this place, and behold! **I have brought the first fruit**."

Joseph Died

What is the role of personal relationships and intergroup dialogue in avoiding, stopping, or repairing harm between communities? The earliest verses of Exodus offer food for thought. First a wide-brush view:

1A) Joseph has a life and relationships in *Mitzrayim,* but
1B) it is not clear to what extent that is true of his brothers' families.

2A) Joseph and his generation die (Ex 1:6); immediately afterward,
2B) the *Yisrael-ites* increase and fill the land (Ex 1:7), with *Yisrael-ite* women birthing so quickly there is no time for the midwives to attend (Ex 1:19).

3A) "A new king arose who didn't know Joseph" (Ex 1:8), and immediately
3B) Pharaoh schemes to oppress the *Yisrael-ites* (Ex 1:9ff).

And now, looking closer:

1) We know quite a bit about Joseph, compared to the other brothers. That "already there" is the briefest of recaps for the longest saga in Genesis (37, 39-50; summarized in *Dick Gregory's Bible Tales,* excerpted above).

We know Joseph's career, how he dressed, what he ate, and a little about his wife -- all *Mitzrayim-ite.*

We do get a few glimpses of the brothers, but even Judah -- whose name will become eponymous with the nation over time -- only gets a substantial role in one chapter (Gen 38).

Jacob's death speech (Gen 49), mentioning each brother, is set within the story of Joseph's leadership in *Mitzrayim.*

2) One generation dies -- or maybe it's really all about the death of Joseph, the only person named in the verse -- and the *Yisrael-ites* are suddenly

---

The story of Judah and Tamar (Gen 38) interrupts Joseph's story. It's a powerful story on its own and one of the few that features a woman as protagonist. It also highlights the crucial role of outsiders – Tamar is Canaanite – in development of the clan that eventually becomes the *Yisrael-ites,* and, ultimately, one branch of the Messianic line. In addition, the story serves literary functions in the larger Joseph arc.

The tale of Jacob's death emphasizes Joseph's role in his father's funeral rites. Joseph arranges both embalming, a *Mitzrayim-ite* practice, with 40 days of mourning in the land where they'd been living, and burial "back home."

NOTE: Jacob's funeral rites are an interfaith/intercultural production.

---

nameless and non-individuated, almost inhuman: a fertile pack spreading out across the land.

3) In the much-noted verse pair, we see a Pharaoh who doesn't know Joseph and the immediate start of terrible brutality and oppression.

Discussing this verse pair, R' Daniel J. Moskovitz asks:

> Does the text mean to suggest that it was the memory of Joseph that had kept the [*Yisrael-ites*] safe from oppression in [*Mitzrayim*]? In other words, was the hatred always there just below the surface, waiting for the opportunity to arise?
> -- "Pharaoh Didn't Know Joseph," commentary provided by Union for Reform Judaism, at MyJewishLearning.com

The question's phrasing seems to cry out for Perry Mason (or some other fictional attorney) to jump up and shout, "Objection. Leading!" But I do think we can profitably consider this question in the context of attempts at dialogue across community divides.

Dam or Bridge

Joseph's relationship to *Mitzrayim-ite* life and government looms much larger than that of his brothers, and his role as a bridge between his extended family and the surrounding culture is highlighted in Genesis. Is it possible, though, that Joseph was the only link between the two groups? Or that his role was so crucial that all collapsed without him?

Attributing all that power to one person makes Joseph seem reminiscent of an organized crime leader or "the Boss" of a political patronage machine, like Chicago Mayor Richard **J.** Daley (1902-76, *z"l*). Is the text suggesting that Joseph, or his memory, kept a lid on intergroup animosity through doling out of protection, jobs, and essential resources?

This is not inconsistent with Joseph's story in Genesis.

It also resembles the contemporary strategy of relying on one big name with known ties to a particular group -- a prominent clergy person, or a screen celebrity, for example -- for entrée to a whole community or as a way of signaling "understanding" after some kind of harm has occurred. (Visiting Sylvia's restaurant in Harlem with Rev. Al Sharpton, or joining a high-profile Passover Seder come to mind.)

Beyond optics, though, what is the power of a single relationship in intergroup understanding?

One relationship can be the source of some education, illuminating past harm and helping to avoid further hateful incidents. One relationship can also serve some conflict-calming functions, helping to keep misunderstanding and anger from snowballing. But, can a single relationship -- or even a bunch of them -- reduce the kind of endemic hatred that R' Moskovitz suggests is "always there just below the surface"? And what, if any, impact can individual relationships have on systemic racism and oppression?

Thin Human Line

Once Exodus begins, the condensed narration emphasizes Joseph's role even more strongly. Causality is never explicit, and yet: Joseph dies, and his People lose their humanity; Pharaoh doesn't know Joseph, and all hell breaks loose. Was Joseph somehow a lone, thin human line preventing genocide?

R' Moskovitz concludes "Pharaoh Didn't Know Joseph" with a shift from Joseph, as an individual, to Joseph as stand-in for an entire community's commitment to the larger society:

> In the case of Joseph, how might things have gone differently had the [*Yisrael-ites*] better guarded and remembered him and his contribution? Nowhere in the text do we read of how they expended their political capital to fend off Pharaoh's harsh decree. The community had not renewed its engagement in [*Mitzrayim-ite*] society: It had not built political bridges, developed new leadership, woven themselves into the fabric of society beyond being a labor force; it was therefore ripe for exploitation.
>
> It is a reminder for every generation of the commandment *al tifrosh min hatzibor* ("Don't separate yourself from the community"). This is not only a commandment to the individual Jew with regard to the Jewish community but also to the Jewish community as a whole not to grow too distant from the society in which it lives and works.

The idea that "the community had not renewed its engagement" highlights a number of issues crucial in exploring the value of intergroup dialogue. Each takes us back to one of the three times Joseph is mentioned at the start of Exodus.

"Pharaoh Didn't Know Joseph," written by R' Daniel J. Moskovitz, is posted at MyJewishLearning.com and attributed as "provided by the Union for Reform Judaism." The piece can be read in full here: tinyurl.com/4d7vpcm3 (or just search at My Jewish Learning).

My Jewish Learning does not date their entries, but several clues suggest that this piece is at least 10 years old. R' Moskovitz is now Senior Rabbi of Temple Sholom in Vancouver, BC.

Many remarks here are in opposition to viewpoints expressed in "Pharaoh Didn't Know Joseph," so this is just a note of appreciation for the piece, which provided much food for thought.

"Just Show Up" and its Cost

This commentary suggests that engagement is the job of the minority community and that it's a straightforward matter, easily accomplished.

Even the biblical evidence raises doubts on this matter, however: Joseph spent all of his adult years in *Mitzrayim* and is portrayed as fully integrated into, and a leader in, the larger society; it is not clear to what extent that was even an option for his brothers, who are portrayed, throughout Genesis, as Other within the larger society. And how does "just show up," promoting participation in many sectors, work for Others today?

Costs of Showing Up

Case 1: DC is home to members of many minority religious groups, plus atheists and people who don't identify with any faith community. Nonetheless, many organizations, even some official bodies, are functionally Christian -- not just a prayer, here or there, in the name of Jesus, but regular reference to Christian faith as an operating principle. In addition, important civic meetings are regularly scheduled on major religious holidays.

Non-Christians can, religious observance permitting, "just show up," and quietly participate in Christian activities masquerading as civic ones. Or we can make a point of noting that the Christian framework is inappropriate, for us and/or for a civic body. We can explain that the crucial Town Hall scheduled for Rosh Hashanah or the event planned for Eid al-Fitr excludes us. Or we can decide to conserve our energy and just drift away.

Whatever choices we make, non-Christians face different costs than folks who are in the majority in attempting to engage. It's exhausting, in some cases illegal, and a constant reminder that we don't entirely belong. But it's not potentially lethal or soul-crushin

Case 2: In 2010, a DC-based group held an interdenominational, women-led service designed for cross-community Jewish participation; some of

that diversity appears in this photo (L-to-R): havurah member (tallit, no head covering); Modern Orthodox (reading Torah; hat, no tallit); then-Reform (kippah and tallit, as gabbai); Conservative (tallit, no head covering). Two women are white-gray-haired, two blond-ish; three of the women are white, and one is Black.

Three years later, *Forward* and *JTA* (Jewish wire service) used this photo, captioned: "A non-Jewish woman is among those at a Torah reading....," to illustrate interfaith worship.

Women pictured who complained publicly to the *Forward* asked: "Which of us do you think is not Jewish?"

Upon complaint -- from those pictured and others, including the congregation erroneously identified as hosting an interfaith Torah reading -- the photo was removed from a story where it did not belong. Without apology or correction.

Given that neither the *Forward* nor JTA issued a correction, we must guess how the error happened. Sabrina Sojourner (above, second from right) was not surprised. Even at synagogues where she was a member or regular visitor, she had been mistaken for Christian clergy or for kitchen staff -- no matter how

"Which of us do you think is not Jewish?" resonates with sad irony because participation and leadership in services, particularly the honors of blessing and reading from the Torah, have been denied women in some Jewish communities in the lifetimes of all those pictured.

In another complicated irony, the congregation pictured does not give non-Jews the Torah honors pictured ...so this photo, what it depicts and how it was used, raise myriad complexities about how "showing up" works and doesn't.

Jewishly she is garbed -- and asked "how are you Jewish?!" (a question Jews of Color hear so often that it inspired MaNishtana's book, *Fine, thanks, how are you, Jewish?*).

It happens that this incident was documented. But Jews of Color face such narrow-minded assumptions when engaging all the time. Black Jews in particular are regularly harassed by synagogue security or "greeters" taught to suspect anyone who "might not belong," and -- in one Brooklyn case -- attacked for carrying a Torah scroll. Many Jews of Color find this treatment enough to drive them away from Jewish life, at least temporarily.

Sabrina Sojourner, now a Jewish chaplain and spiritual leader, recently taught:

> We, Jews of Color, Multicultural-Multiracial-Multi-Ethnic, Indigenous, Sephardic, Persian, and Mizrahi Jews – each and all of us who do not fit the mold, the lie – many to most of you were carefully taught about who is and who is not Jewish, need you....to crack open and destroy every stereotype you hold about any and all of us who you perceive to be different from you, including those of us with disabilities, identify as lesbian, gay, bisexual, queer, non-binary, transgender, questioning, and so much more.
> -- "Some are Guilty, but All are Responsible," remarks on Kabbalat Shabbat at Kol Shalom (Rockville, MD)

Sojourner notes that Jews of all backgrounds and appearances "want you not to be surprised or suspicious when we show-up" for worship or activities. She adds that Jews of Color and others "who do not fit the mold" have deep need of spiritual homes precisely "because living within this skin is sometimes just too much."

> We need our spiritual homes to be a place where we can go and be seen, loved, comforted, consoled, soothed, celebrated, and honored because living within this skin is sometimes just too much. Daily, we can experience the stress of spiritual, emotional, intellectual, and sometimes physical abuse for no other reason than we exist and are obviously different.
> -- "Some are Guilty..." shared on SabrinaSojourner.net

Case 3: History offers no shortage of instances in which minority group involvement with the larger society has met with opposition, sometimes violent. Reconstruction in the U.S. precisely exemplifies an attempt to build bridges and foster engagement across communities: the resulting opposition was enormous and often deadly.

It was during this backlash that DC's local government, which included Black office-holders, was overthrown by Congress in 1871. Explaining why he took this step, Rep. John Tyler Morgan, "a plantation owner and Ku Klux Klan leader... said: 'it was necessary to burn down the barn to get rid of the rats'" (from DC 101 history, more below).

Reconstruction and DC history may not exactly parallel attempts by Joseph's brothers and their descendants to engage in *Mitzrayim-ite* society, but failures and dangers of the "just show up" model in history suggest that engaging with the larger society would not necessarily have prevented exploitation.

And, to return to Sabrina Sojourner's remarks quoted above and paraphrase her call: It is the job of those in the majority, those with more power in the situation, to do the work of destroying stereotypes and making "just show up" a safe possibility for all.

Ripe for Exploitation

As noted, "Pharaoh Didn't Know Joseph" suggests that the *Yisrael-ites* were "ripe for exploitation," due to their own lack of engagement:

> The community had not...built political bridges, developed new leadership, woven themselves into the fabric of society beyond being a labor force; it was therefore ripe for exploitation.

This suggestion seems to imagine two communities of equal status, somehow segregated by (mutual?) choice but participating in the same economic and civic life. History probably includes some examples, but this author cannot think of any in which the power dynamics did not favor one community or any in which respectability politics avoided exploitation.

Moreover, Exodus itself seems to suggest something starker, less equal, and not at all mutual: One generation dies (Ex 1:6), and the *Yisrael-ites* are suddenly nameless and non-individuated, almost inhuman: a fertile pack spreading out across the land (Ex 1:7, 19). Perhaps the suggestion is that engagement earlier in the story might have prevented this dehumanization, given the warning, in current times, "to the Jewish community as a whole not to grow too distant from the society in which it lives and works."

And that leads us back to intergroup dialogue and other attempts to "humanize" or prevent exploitation through contact.

Humanizing and Dehumanizing

Pharaoh's attempts to get rid of, or rein in, the *Yisrael-ites* take an even more dramatic turn as Exodus Chapter 1 closes:

> Then Pharaoh charged all his people saying: "Every boy that is born you shall throw into the river..." (Ex 1:22).

Can we imagine any people behaving as Pharaoh directs toward *Yisrael-ite* babies? Such extreme behavior is hard to fathom...

until we recall the Atlantic Slave Trade and its on-going aftermath....
or Europe's treatment of the Roma.
or the Trail of Tears in U.S. history.
or colonial treatment of black and brown people.
or violent suppression of LGBTQ people through the ages.
or differences in response in different areas, based on race and other factors, at time of natural disaster -- or pandemic.
All that is needed is a framework that allows some humans to dehumanize other humans -- or, even more simply, to put interests of those they hold closer and dearer above more distant Others.

One reaction to this reality is the impulse to facilitate introductions of one kind or another, on the theory that no one could possibly treat another group so badly if only they knew those Others...or some of them. This impulse, in some ways, was at the heart of Cross River Dialogue. It is also a factor in much journalism and so many issue campaigns....

Hadiya and "Humanizing"

For years before Cross River Dialogue came into being, I struggled with the gap between my places of work and residence, where gun violence is regular, and places of worship where gun violence is rare and was then rarely mentioned. Attempting to put faces to statistics, back in 2013, I suggested to clergy at one DC congregation (one, it happens, with a strong connection to the city of Chicago) focusing on Hadiya Pendleton, a 15-year-old Chicagoan gunned down (1/29/13), shortly after participating in Obama's second Inauguration parade.

From three of my remarks before mourners' kaddish:

2013

Hadiya Z. Pendleton liked Fig Newtons and performed in a drill team that participated in Obama's 2013 Inaugural parade. She lived in the Kenwood neighborhood of Chicago, not far from where I lived for several years and where friends still live, not far from the Obama family home. She never reached her 16th birthday, which would have been on June 2. She was gunned down on January 29 [2013], in a public park at 45th & Drexel, apparently caught in a gang-related shooting.

Our segregated lives mean many of us do not personally know young people killed in street violence (or in military, for that matter). I once lived only blocks from the park where Hadiya was killed, e.g., but rarely visited the area between 43rd and 47th streets. I know many residents of DC who, similarly, rarely cross an intersection where shootings are an all-too-regular fact of life.

Therefore, I ask those relatively untouched by the violence that besets too many of our neighborhoods and robs too many of our fellow citizens of their childhoods, if not their lives, to take Hadiya Pendleton's life into their hearts and mourn her passing. Today, I ask others to join me in recognizing Hadiya Pendleton as a teacher.

Hadiya's life teaches how much can be packed into just a few years. Her death reminds us of the fragility of life at any age and about the duty of elders to protect our youth. Some Jews recite kaddish when a teacher dies, and I encourage others to join me in doing so. May her memory be for a blessing, and may that blessing include a renewed commitment to make our cities safe places for young life.

2014

...She liked Fig Newtons, my favorite snack when I was a teenager. She and I both visited Washington, DC, while still in high school — I was part of Washington Workshops Congressional Seminars, and she performed in Obama's Inaugural parade. Both of us participated in local anti-crime initiatives: "Operation Whistle Stop" in my case; and a "Think Smart" anti-gang video in hers.

"Hadiya Pendleton was me, and I was her," Michelle Obama last April . "But I got to grow up, and go to Princeton and Harvard Law School, and have a career and a family and the most blessed life I could ever imagine. And Hadiya? Oh, we know that story…." ("Working Together to Address Youth Violence," 4/10/13, on Obama White House Archives)

Hadiya Pendleton was gunned down on January 29, 2013, shot to death in a public park because, from the back, she resembled someone associated with a gang. Hadiya never reached her 16th birthday, which would have been June 2, 2013.

While there are obvious differences between my life and both Hadiya Pendleton's and Michelle Obama's, my reaction to Hadiya's death was similar to Mrs. Obama's. She rightly points out how just a few urban blocks can mean the difference between a life rich in possibility and one circumscribed by need and loss. I would add that we cannot allow those few blocks – or even a few miles – to insulate us from our neighbors' grief.

Since last January [so 2013-14], the District of Columbia has lost ten teenagers to gunshots, but I do not usually hear their names read from this *bima* [podium]. I know many who mourn for young people killed on DC streets, but my own children graduated high school without losing an immediate friend to that plague, and neither child remembers the frequent gunshots of their toddler years, so they grew up without that fear. The relative segregation of our lives mean that many of us here today are not directly touched by the violence that robs too many of our neighbors of childhoods. But Judaism forbids us from standing idly by the blood of a sister. And *Shabbat Zachor* [Remember!], just before Purim, calls us to remember the threat of Amalek, who attacked the hungry, weary stragglers among the Israelites in the desert (Deut. 25:17-19).

In Chicago, DC, and other cities, whole neighborhoods like Hadiya's have become stragglers on the road out of bondage, filled with youth who are hungry and weary and, all too often, vulnerable to attack. Until all teens like Hadiya can safely hang out in the local parks, we have failed to blot out the name of Amalek....

2016

These remarks were offered in honor of what would have been Hadiya Pendleton's 19th birthday.

> The next day, Kyra was back in gym class. As always. The teacher was taking attendance. As always. As he proceeded through the alphabet toward the P's, she wondered: Would he call Hadiya Pendleton?

> When he didn't, students cried.

> ...And like the rest of Hadiya's friends, Kyra counted the Tuesdays since Hadiya died.

> Tuesday, week one.
> Tuesday, week two.
> Tuesday, week three.... ....

> ...[The three teens no longer saw each other regularly when they met up in spring 2013.] It was, coincidentally, the 13th Tuesday after Hadiya's death, but they don't count Tuesdays so much

anymore. They count months. Monday made three months.
— Jennifer Delgado, Bridget Doyle and Mary Schmich,
"Life After Hadiya," Chicago Tribune

The article's time-counting motif seems fitting for the period of the Omer, when we enumerate the days and the weeks between Passover and Shavuot. June 4, for example, was 42 days of the Omer, making six weeks. Some would also call it the day of *malchut b'yesod* — translated as something like "nobility in bonding" — based on a mystical counting system.

Similarly, the losses associated with Hadiya's death were reckoned in small and large ways – in gym class and in long-term desolation — as well as in ways harder to express.

"That bullet did a lot more than just kill my baby," Cleopatra Cowley-Pendleton has said.

But we can also count the ways, small and large and harder to express, that Hadiya's bright spark continues to inspire conversation and thought, prayer and action. The toll of shootings like Hadiya's — psychologically, economically, educationally, and otherwise — is staggering. But the blessing of her memory is enormous, too.

When these remarks were offered in 2016, the congregation, like quite a few at that time, was marking "Wear Orange" for gun violence prevention. The campaign -- originally a personal tribute to Hadiya by her friends and a call for safety for kids like them -- had by then been adopted, and substantially changed, by Moms Demand Action (another story).

Each set of remarks generated response from congregants, and I felt less isolated in my grief around local gun violence. But were we creating genuine links between those more isolated from the carnage and those more directly suffering?

Value of Bridges?

Meanwhile, in 2015 I wrote for Reform Judaism blog:

Metrobus carries me between my home in the Southeast quadrant...and Temple Micah in the city's Northwest quadrant. Metrobus also carries me to work across the District's geographic, demographic, and existential dividing line, the Anacostia River.

For decades, I have struggled with the river divide: on one side, communities affected by violence, its causes and aftermath, grief and mourning; on the other, communities privileged to work and worship in relative calm. On one side, Christian and African traditions; on the other, a diversity of worship, including a smattering of synagogues.

And me, traveling between the two, carrying strangeness, and its loneliness, with me.

In the past year, heartbreaking circumstances have helped foster a new sense of connection, one I hope will continue to grow... [After my colleague's murder in May 2015, Temple Micah began listing the names of all DC homicide victims before mourners' kaddish.]

When I witnessed a gun homicide a few weeks later, it was a great help to know I would not be alone in my grief when I arrived, still shattered, at Shabbat services. Without that new bridge supporting me, I am not sure I could have traveled the river divide that week.

...Reciting the names of those killed helps make visible parts of our city's tapestry that can be obscured, depending on the view. This is having an effect, fellow congregants tell me....

Span of Our Bridges

For a time, strangers (who didn't know I'd helped instigate it) mentioned the power of the homicide list. For a time, I wrote related meditations and prayers. This one, offered "with special intention for the healing of [neighborhoods] rocked by persistent violence," is based on "*Mah Tovu*," regularly sung to open prayers at Temple Micah, and Psalm 30 (not in the Reform prayer book but a favorite of mine):

Kavanah (intention) for morning prayers (8/21/15):

How lovely are these tents!
not far from housing that has seen better days and housing that has seen too
many awful ones.

I love the place of Your house, reached through streets
collecting cigarette butts, the odd chicken wing, echoes of homicide.

Through Your abundant love, I enter Your house,
where these peaceful walls remind us: "If I am for myself alone, what am I?"
while a few miles away homes reel from gunshots and mourning,
makeshift memorials of teddy bears and candles pooled with tears and rain.
Meetings and vigils and "let this be the last."

My prayer seeks a favorable time —
Does joy come in the morning, where weeping has not tarried for the night?
Can we dance together, if we have not yet joined in lament?

You answer with your saving truth:
Your glory's dwelling-place spans mountain top and pit.
We are shaken and we stand firm.
Remove our sackcloth and dress us to praise You, Source of Healing and Help.

For a time, the congregation had an active Gun Violence Prevention Working Group, which grew from a new assistant rabbi's reaction to hearing that list of names and the strong involvement of a few others. The rabbi has since moved on; the group is less active....

Mourning: Humanizing and Being Human

Over the the last few pages, we've considered possibilities for mourning in building empathy and spurring social action. But sometimes we need space -- as Jews or as part of other communities -- for individual and collective grief, around realities with a political edge. (Period).

Alas! How lonely sits the city
once great with joyful people!
New horrors fill horizons now
while old pain never left
Each new loss diminishes
the streets themselves bereft.

"*Eichah* for My City and Maybe Yours" arose from a mismatch of sentiment: Jews in DC, as around the country, were using Tisha B'av to focus on refugees, while few seemed to notice regular, deep grief right nearby: Just five days before Tisha B'av 2018, 10-year-old Makiyah Wilson had been shot to death around the corner from me. My original lament read:

> Tisha B'av [literally: "ninth day of the month of Av"], the lowest day of the Jewish year, marks destruction of the Temple and other sad history, with some communities mourning current events as well. The acrostic *Eichah* [Lamentations] is read. "*Eichah* for My City and Maybe Yours" is based loosely on that lament.

Refugees are some, just some,
of misery's many faces

Once mourning is linked to action, questions of strategy and efficacy arise. A national call for action on immigration makes sense for a group of Jews -- especially those who can easily gather on the lawn just feet from the White House fence -- to join. Moreover, immigration is an issue that resonates with many Jews. And, of course, we cannot make grief a competition.

But cross-community dialogue might lead us to ask: Where is the wailing and strategizing for the many non-refugees in cages? Is it appropriate to gather for mourning inside DC and treat local concerns as background noise, sparing neither tear nor prayer for the city around us?

On the one hand, it seems hard to divorce some grief from action: Can we mourn for individuals who died unhoused, without addressing conditions that left people outside? Can we mark life lost to police violence, apart from grief around conditions and systems that permitted that death? On the other hand: Might we just sit and weep for all the families traumatized by incarceration? Join together in wailing for failures of our education system? Mark victims of gun violence without an action follow up?

Failing to recognize community members' grief can be devastating and isolating, and yet our communities encompass such a wide variety of concerns that addressing one cause can leave those focused elsewhere feeling bereft. Touching on every area of concern could be overwhelming. Might a generalized mourning practice be needed?

Meanwhile, the Jewish calendar is already filled with fast days, and the Omer is observed by many Jews as a time of semi-mourning
-- Do we need more?

Bitterly we weep all night
cheeks wet with tears unseen
If we are to join together,
we must widen this choir of woe
When some cries are background noise
what's the meaning of "friend" and "foe"?

City crying out with loss:
six-year-old child shot to death
joining a list, far too long,
of youth killed in past years.
Community grief so deep for some
while others escape most tears.

Down our roads, more peril
desolation, violence, fear
systems that crush and jail
separate, cage, and hate
Borders come in many shapes
Too often closed, that welcome gate

Evidence mounts. But do we act?
ICE camps remain; racism persists.
Policing prospers, yet safety eludes
Some thrive, while too many do without.
Must we ignore some of our truths
in chasing a joint goal to shout?

Forging coalition is struggle, tougher in anguish.
Inside affliction, can we hear another cry?
It is painful and complex, but we must keep trying
trying to heed the whole sound
I know you can hear it, God once declared loudly:
that voice of a sibling crying up from the ground
-- "Eichah for My City and Maybe Yours"

If we do not grieve, what are we?
If we cannot grieve and still act, who will?

Memory, People, Place

In terms of plot, we are not plowing along in the Exodus narrative at a very swift pace. Slowing down the narrative allows us to explore characters and the lay of the land in new ways. It also allows us to look at the impact of some moments that we usually slide past. These are crucial elements in truly REreading the text. Not coincidentally, these same shifts in thinking are also crucial to intergroup dialogue.

Our collaborations are frequently built around a specific goal. For example

an election campaign;

budget season priorities;

opposition to worrisome legislation or troublesome agency action;

fund-raising for an urgent need; and/or

raising awareness around particular concerns.

Slowing down to really explore who is in the room, where meetings are situated, and the impact of basic interactions can seem so much less urgent than work is immediately in front of us. But building better, more equitable communities requires that pause.

...I once read that the stories of F. Scott Fitzgerald (1896-1940) share so many similarities because he kept writing the story of his relationship with his wife Zelda, over and over again, hoping it would result in a different ending. A related African proverb, a favorite of Kymone Freeman, tells us: "Until the lions have their historians; the tales of the hunt will continue to glorify the hunters."

....To accomplish valuable intergroup learning, with an aim toward trans-forming power relationships and resource distribution, we need to know our stories -- our own, those of our neighbors, and those in our history and lore -- in new ways.

Guarding and Remembering

Returning again to "Pharaoh Didn't Know Joseph," Moskovitz asks: "In the case of Joseph, how might things have gone differently had the [*Yisrael-ites*] better guarded and remembered him and his contribution?" Later we'll look in more detail at Joseph's story. Here, though, R' Moskovitz is actually talking about guarding "the blessed memory of those who came before us" in a non-biblical sense. This is a crucial obligation that is too often completely botched in the context of intergroup relations.

Consider the famous, regularly twisted examples of Rev. Dr. Martin Luther King Jr and R' Abraham Joshua Heschel. Their individual legacies are often distorted, as is their work together, symbolized by that picture of the two of them, in a line of lei-wearing marchers, leaving Selma for Montgomery.

Marc Dollinger discusses that photo's misuse in *Black Power, Jewish Politics*:

> The iconic image of Rabbi Abraham Joshua Heschel marching alongside Dr. Martin Luther King Jr. in Selma symbolized the highest ideals of an interracial, interfaith movement that testified to the essential similarities between blacks and Jews. This filiopietistic* read on Jewish liberal activism encouraged the construction of a false narrative that congratulated Jews for their social justice passion and criticized Black Power for undoing the good work of early civil rights workers." -- Marc Dollinger, *Black Power, Jewish Politics*

> * "of or relating to an often excessive veneration of ancestors or tradition" – Merriam-Webster on-line
> Sharing because I had to look up this very apt term, not in my 1939 OED or 1963 Funk & Wagnalls

Dollinger's entire book might be considered an elaboration of that single paragraph, so I won't try to summarize but instead recommend reading and carefully considering.

Heschel and His Praying Legs

In addition to feeding the narrative that Dollinger describes above, some famous words about Selma from R' Abraham Joshua Heschel (1907-1972) are regularly used to promote many misunderstandings:

> For many of us the march from Selma to Montgomery was about protest and prayer. Legs are not lips and walking is not kneeling. And yet our legs uttered songs. Even without words, our march was worship. I felt my legs were praying.

AJH's praying-legs are often cited in context of activities that are safe for participants, including marches protected, even escorted, by police. In Selma, however, earlier marchers were beaten by police, leaving 25-year-old John Lewis near death. (Rep. Lewis, 1940-2020, was then an organizer for SNCC [Students Nonviolent Coordinating Committee].) The demonstration itself was responding to the murder of Jimmie Lee Jackson, killed by a State Trooper after a peaceful voting rights march on Feb. 26. Although federal troops did eventually step in for the third crossing attempt and protect the demonstrators, when AJH and others arrived on Mar 21, they had no expectation of protection. Using his words without nuanced recollection erases at least two crucial factors.

First: real risk. The march Heschel participated in, alongside King and others, was a dangerous undertaking, requiring commitment to nonviolence in the face of harassment and possible violence. It was not a safe and demonstration in which participants expect to be protected, if not escorted, by police. (Also please note that AJH was not substituting civic activity for his usual observance of Shabbat and did not advocate that.)

Second: difference in risk. While everyone in the march was at risk, they faced far different treatment once they stepped away from the demonstration. Heschel was no stranger to horror: He grew up in Poland, studied in Germany, and lived through the destruction of Europe's Jewish communities. By 1965, however, AJH resided in the northern U.S., where his relatively prestigious teaching job and his white skin provided a measure of protection and respect that King and many others in that march would never know.

Other distortions: Prior to Selma, AJH and MLK had known one another for several years. AJH was invited to join MLK in Selma; he didn't just turn up for his own reasons.

Sabbath/Festival and Action

For many Jews the question of whether to take part in action on the sabbath or a festival does not arise at all: either because their observance prohibits related activities (driving or using transit, carrying anything, including money, etc.) or because their observance doesn't include those restrictions. Individual Jews and organizations make participation decisions in many ways. But honoring AJH's memory means **not** using his words (about a Sunday activity, BTW) as precedence.

On the other hand, we have the teaching of Esther Ticktin, *z"l*, of Fabrangen Havurah (DC). She is credited with ending an argument about whether attending an anti-Vietnam War march on a Saturday could be considered *"pikuach nefesh,"* a case in which saving a life takes precedence over other duties (like sabbath observance). Esther's conclusion: Attending is a violation of Shabbat, in community understanding, but going anyway underlines its urgency and import.

Within Judaism, many confuse AJH's political positions (which some consider "far left") with liberal theology and practice. Nor was every Jew of his time on board the fact that he was taking political -- some would say "prophetic" -- stances at all or with the content of his activism, especially around the war in Viet Nam.

Some additional memories of import:
While the lei-wearing photo seems to be on everyone's website, it's harder to find recollections of the March 9 protest in New York City. Heschel joined with SNCC and CORE (Congress for Racial Equity) activists, protesting treatment of the earlier (Selma demonstrators -- on what became known as "Bloody Sunday" -- and calling for arrest of those who'd participated in the police riot. AJH helped lead a crowd of 800 to FBI Headquarters. That effort -- and others of SNCC and CORE -- helped pave the way for the successful Selma to Montgomery march later in the month. This incident landed Heschel on the FBI watch list.

Guarding AJH's memory in the context of intergroup dynamics would mean taking to heart -- finally, after nearly 60 years -- his call for worship communities to acknowledge failures and repent: "We forfeit the right to worship God as long as we continue to humiliate Negroes" (AJH telegram to President John F. Kennedy, 7/16/63). It would mean finally making changes based on his his teachings:

> Perhaps this Conference should have been called "Religion or Race." You cannot worship God and at the same time look at man as if he were a horse....

> ...What is an idol? Any god who is mine but not yours, any god concerned with me but not with you, is an idol.
> -- Conference on "Religion and Race" (1/14/63)

King, Remembered and Not

Misuses of Martin Luther King Jr's memory have reached an all-time, outrageous low with recent attempts to undermine education in the U.S. history by means of the aspirational "content of their character." But misuses of MLK are not new and are not limited to this egregious campaign to outlaw mention of race.

For decades, we heard about love driving out hate but not "the 'congenital deformity' of racism that has crippled the nation from its inception."

And somehow, we forget:

> For the vast majority of white Americans, the past decade [1950s to early 1960s] —the first phase—had been a struggle to treat the

Negro with a degree of decency, not equality. White America was ready to demand that the Negro should be spared the lash of brutality and coarse degradation, but it had never been truly committed to helping him out of poverty, exploitation or all forms of discrimination. The outraged white citizen had been sincere when he snatched the whips from the Southern sheriffsWhite Americans left the Negro on the ground and in devastating numbers walked off with the aggressor. It appeared that the White segregationist and the ordinary White citizen had more in common with one another than either had with the Negro.

— *Where Do We Go From Here: Chaos or Community?* 1967;

We've managed to divorce "the Beloved Community" from its context: "The triple evils of poverty, racism, and militarism are forms of violence that exist in a vicious cycle. They are interrelated, all-inclusive, and stand as barriers to our living in the Beloved Community."

In the spring of 1968, MLK was in Washington DC to introduce the upcoming Poor People's Campaign. In addition to addressing the roots of racism and the need for "something positive and massive in order to get rid of all the effects of racism and the tragedies of racial injustice," he spoke of the "gulf between the haves and the have-nots" in the U.S., the need for "an alternative to war and bloodshed," and the link between militarism and poverty. ("Remaining Awake Through a Great Revolution," National Cathedral, 3/31/68). He was assassinated four days later.

If we are guarding the memory of MLK, as a leader from a minority community relating to the larger society, we must have his whole legacy in mind...including criticism of his early ministry and objections to his later preaching -- from in- and outside his own community -- as well as complex interactions with other Black leaders, various Christian groups, and a host of other sources.

The Bible text is not explicit, but Joseph likely had detractors, within the larger family of Jacob as well as in other parts of *Mitzrayim-ite* society. Joseph faced risks, including indefinite imprisonment (for a crime he didn't commit). Similarly, perhaps, guarding and remembering MLK and AJH as examples, together and apart, of leaders who contributed to intergroup relations in the past is not a simple matter.

23

Don't Mute Joseph

Returning to the text of early Exodus:

> A new king arose over [*Mitzrayim*], who did not know Joseph. He said to his people, "Look, [the *Yisrael-ite*] people are more numerous and stronger than we. Come let us deal shrewdly with them, so that they do not increase; otherwise, in event of a war, they might join our enemies in fighting against us and rise up from the ground." -- Ex 1:8-10

Although trouble begins when Joseph dies, many commentators focus on the "not knowing." In "Rereading the Plagues," David Silber writes:

> Pharaoh's "not knowing" carries with it a sense of ingratitude, as Joseph was the savior of his nation; it also suggests callousness and a lack of sensitivity, and the Torah implies that it is not just an intellectual lapse but a moral deficiency.
> --p.56, *Go Forth and Learn: A Passover Haggadah*

In a similar spirit, not knowing the contributions of enslaved and otherwise oppressed people to U.S. history "carries with it a sense of ingratitude." And not understanding the cost of such contributions "suggests callousness and a lack of sensitivity." As in the Exodus story, this is "not just an intellectual lapse but a moral deficiency."

Without trying to address the enormous topic of how history is and isn't taught in the U.S., awareness of "not knowing" as a "moral deficiency" should compel all of us to learn something new about our history. Maybe something national -- like the history of "whiteness" as a legal property -- or maybe something hyperlocal, like who owned the house on the corner in previous generations or what restaurants have come and gone before your favorite moved in.

Keep in mind the idea that Pharaoh's not-knowing caused generations of pain followed by cataclysm. Work to repair not-knowing wherever possible.

Don't Mute DC

Whatever your association with DC, passing familiarity with the life and culture of people who live in the city many view as "the nation's capitol," is essential. One place to start is with the "Don't Mute DC" movement.

Several CRD participants were active at the height of the Don't Mute DC movement, in the Before Times (when the first version of this book was in process). Cross River Dialoguer Ronald Moten is considered co-founder of the effort and is now director of DC's new Go-Go Museum -- a circumstance that was brought about in part by an attack on Go-Go music and an enormous display of not-knowing on the part of some newer city residents.

In 2019, a battle erupted over music and public space at an intersection of long-standing culture, exemplified by a corner store playing loud Go-Go music, and new luxury, exemplified by relatively new condo residents complaining about noise. Julien Broomfield, then a Howard University senior, created the hashtag #DontMuteDC, and a movement celebrating DC's signature music and culture developed.

To understand anything at all about this story, it is helpful to begin with this:

> Go-Go is more than just music. It's a complex expression of cultural values masquerading in the guise of party music in our nation's capitol. -- *The Beat: Go-Go's Fusion of Funk and Hip-Hop* (2009)

Anyone who lives or works in DC -- or has an interest in the nation's capital -- should know something about Go-Go. Check out current offerings of the Go-Go Museum and/or look at history through the above-cited book, Ayanna Long' movie "The Let Out," and Dr. Natalie Hopkinson's *Go-Go Live: The Musical Live and Death of a Chocolate City.*

Many new DC residents don't know, or connect to, DC's history in general and, more specifically, to "Chocolate City." Aspects of local culture, including drummers and other street musicians, become focal points for conflict between residents and businesses. These conflicts often pit longer-term and newer DC folks against one another.

NOTE: Not every native or long-time DC resident is, or was, a Go-Go fan -- despite its declaration as the city's "official music."

"Chocolate City"
In 1975, the funk band Parliament released the album, "Chocolate City." Its title song references DC's status -- at the time -- as a majority Black city, honoring its Black culture and leadership:

> ...There's a lot of chocolate cities, around
> We've got Newark, we've got Gary
> Somebody told me we got L.A
> And we're working on Atlanta
>
> ...The last percentage count was eighty
> You don't need the bullet when you got the ballot
> Are you up for the downstroke, CC?
> Chocolate City
> Are you with me out there?...
> -- George Clinton

Since the 2010 US Census, however, the District has gained nearly 100,000 new residents, many of whom "don't know Joseph."

Results of Don't Mute DC movement so far:

- return of music to the corner;
- designation of Go-Go as "official music" of DC;
- collaborations with Smithsonian and DC Public Libraries to preserve #DontMuteDC- and Go-Go-related material;
- City investment in properties on MLK Avenue, SE, where the new Go-Go Museum is in place and developing programming and exhibits;
- attention to education needs in the Shaw neighborhood and to health care east of the river (home to many of the activists).

Picking up a little Go-Go background or appreciation is a step in addressing the "not knowing" that plagues DC and the country, but it's important to guard against dangerous side-effects of this [word here]

June 2019 Don't Mute DC event on U Street NW

Image: Night-time. Some street-lights glow on a crowd, filling every square foot of space between the glass-fronted building on the northwest corner of U and 14th and older brick buildings along 14th Street. At the center are truck beds where bands and speakers were set up.

Note: The glass-fronted Frank Reeves Center, a city office building, in the above photo looks new in comparison to the other structures. It opened in 1986, when Marion Barry (ז״ל) was mayor, as part of a development plan for a struggling commercial district. Changes along U Street and 14th Street are some of the most pronounced in DC in recent decades. A new round of redevelopment for the same corner is now in the works.

Already There

Two roads to *Mitzrayim* are outlined in the first verses of Exodus:

> Now these are the names of the sons of *Yisrael*, who came into
> *Mitzrayim* with Jacob...
> ...and Joseph was in *Mitzrayim* already -- Exodus 1:1-5

Mitzrayim-ites were, presumably, already in the land for many generations

Joseph's story is long and complex. Over the course of Genesis, he is

- a younger son, eleventh of twelve; his mother, Rachel, died in childbirth with the last of the children, her only other birth-child;

- especially beloved by his father, thought a pest of a dreamer by his brothers;

- sold into servitude in *Mitzrayim*;

- trusted and favored in the household of a *Mitzrayim* official;

- falsely accused of a crime and imprisoned;

- a seasoned interpreter of dreams, released from prison to interpret Pharaoh's dream when others cannot;

- second-in-command to Pharaoh.

Joseph experiences ups and downs personally, with his family of origin, and in his engagements with *Mitzrayim*: arriving as property, "succeeding" in service to a palace household, serving years in prison, and then an exalted service as second in command to Pharaoh.

Through this last position Joseph reunites with his brothers and their families and arranges for the whole clan to settle in *Mitzrayim* during a famine; the family is invited to tend the crown's cattle, and they thrive becoming a sort of proto-nation. The brothers are described as first sojourning, then settling, and finally, acquiring land -- or, perhaps, being grabbed by the land.

During this same famine period, *Mitzrayim-ites* come to Joseph for help; Joseph has shored up resources for Pharaoh in anticipation of the famine -- which Pharaoh had dreamed and Joseph interpreted. *Mitzrayim-ites* first sell their animals to Pharaoh, then their land, finally offering themselves as *avadim* [serfs] in exchange for basic supplies (Gen 47:19).

Thus, Joseph engineers an enormous economic shift across *Mitzrayim* -- seen as a brilliant strategy for managing a deepening famine and/or a huge land- and resource-grab for the crown.

Joseph's ups and downs are essential to the literary and religious themes of the story. There is one constant, however, that cannot be overlooked:

Pharaoh is never down. His power remains unchanged.

Vaguely reminiscent of the Joseph story, DC's history is full of ups and downs and shifting relationships to power and self-determination. The first episode in Serve Your City DC's "DC 101" series, held in January 2021, provided an overview, excerpted next page.

DC 101: Housing and Development

"DC was once the home of the Piscataway and the Nacotchtank people, forced out in 1650." (Reginald Black)

"European colonists enslaved Africans" until April 16 1862. "Slavery was then replaced with a combination of violent, racial terror and legal Jim Crow segregation." (RB)

Lending redlining was used to segregate, and racially restricted covenants that barred the sale or rental of housing to Black people and/or Jews in some areas.

The Federal Housing Authority would not lend to Black people, while white home ownership grew.

"By 1870, Washington DC had evolved a powerful local government, with a mayor and City Council. City Council seats, committees, and jobs were held by many Blacks...The last mayor was Matthew G Emery, who was overthrown by a Southern-controlled Congress in 1871." (James Shabazz)

There was a powerful Statehood movement at that time.

Explaining why he felt it necessary to overthrow the DC government, Rep. John Tyler Morgan, "a plantation owner and Ku Klux Klan leader... said: 'it was necessary to burn down the barn to get rid of the rats.'" (JS)

A Congressional Control Board was established and persisted for decades.

By 1940s, there was a "grass-roots provisional government," with active committees, lawyers, and budgets. Separate associations existed for Black and white residents, but they cooperated on approaches to Congress and succeeded in obtaining resources. "However, the poor, the unemployed, and the homeless Black population lived in rooming house or back-alley Shantytowns" and were ignored or rejected and eventually moved to public housing in "Urban Renewal -- or Negro Removal" efforts. (JS)

By 1972, DC "Home Rule" was established with Advisory Neighborhood Commissions, transferring power of the provisional government.

For 20 years, ANCs were populated by those experienced community leaders. "By 1990, this generation was dead or retired.... " (JS)

-- DC history presented by Reginald Black, co-founder of People for Fairness Coalition among other titles, and James Shabazz, spokesperson for Organized Vendors for Economic Cooperation. Summary includes "direct quotations" and paraphrase.

For this and other episodes of the educational series, look for the "DC 101" playlist on Serve Your City DC's YouTube channel

"The People"

As Pharaoh's chief administrator during a time of famine, Joseph engineers a centralized economy -- with all but the priests of *Mitzrayim* understood as *avadim* [slaves/serfs]. Moreover, Joseph resettles the entire population:

> And as for the people, he removed them city by city, from one end of the border of *Mitzrayim* to the other. -- Gen 47:21

An old commentary says that Joseph did this out of love for his brothers: If everyone was displaced, no one could call his brothers exiles (Talmud Chullin

> The verb in Genesis 47:21, "remove" or "resettle" [he-evir, הֶעֱבִיר], is related to "Hebrew [ivri]" or "boundary-crosser.

60b, ~500 CE, Babylon). Later discussion says the purpose "was to prevent uprisings by populations who had no roots in their countries and therefore had no good reason to start a rebellion" (Rashbam, 12th CE, France, via Sefaria.org).

Rabbi Justin David, formerly a congregational rabbi in DC, writes about Joseph's resettlement strategy and Rashbam's take on it:

> ...we have an explicit condemnation of Joseph from Rabbi Meir ben Shmuel, known as the Rashbam, the grandson of Rashi...The Rashbam compares Joseph not only to the king of Samuel's warnings [1 Sam 7], but also to the autocratic Achashverosh, the Persian king of the Book of Esther, and Sennacherib, the ruthless Assyrian invader (see 2 Kings 18)....

> But ultimately, there are problems with this critical reading of Joseph. Our judgment of Joseph as an exploitative despot does not seem to be borne out by other elements of the biblical text. After all, it is not under Joseph that the people experience excessive suffering, but under the Pharaoh "who did not know Joseph" at the beginning of Exodus. --
> -- "Benevolent Dictatorship or Righteous Balance?" at My Jewish Learning

While R' David lets Joseph off the hook in this essay, he concludes: "We should always be wary of the uses and abuses of institutional power."

Clearly R' David, like much of Jewish commentary, focuses on *Yisrael-ite* suffering; but that's not the whole picture. Doesn't much depend on how we read "the people"? What if we retold the story to include how everyone suffered or thrived?

What if we retold the story to include how everyone suffered or thrived?

A brief pause for acknowledging some deep,
abiding -- and in some cases, on-going -- losses.

International Day for the Commemoration of the Two-Hundredth Anniversary of the Abolition of the Transatlantic Slave Trade

Little is known about the 400-year long transatlantic slave trade and its lasting consequences felt throughout the world, or of the contribution of slaves to the building of the societies of their enslavement. This lack of knowledge has served to marginalize people of African descent across Europe, North America and South America.

The purpose of this Day is to honour the memory of those who died as a result of slavery as well as those who have been exposed to the horrors of the middle passage and have fought for freedom from enslavement. In addition, it is a day to discuss the causes, consequences, and lessons of the transatlantic slave trade in order to raise awareness about the dangers of racism and prejudice

The transatlantic slave trade was unique within the entire history of slavery due to its duration (400 years), its scale (approximately 17 million people excluding those who died during transport) and the legitimization accorded to it, including under laws of the time.
-- UN General Assembly announcement, Dec 17, 2007,
declaring annual commemoration, March 25

Healing the Wounds of Trans-Atlantic Slave Trade and Slavery

The violence of slavery did not end with abolition. Its contemporary consequences are still active in the form of the terrible poison of racism that continues to contaminate societies. Even today, racism kills, discriminates and humiliates....

One of the widest spread and most damaging legacies of the slave trade is racism, institutionalised, cultural and structural, which has repercussions on all continents of our planet, as the basis of xenophobia, discrimination, prejudice and dehumanisation.

Ultimately, healing is a process that addresses the root cause of dehumanisation and remedies its effects. It also includes recognising the structural conditions that dehumanise.
-- *Healing the Wounds of Trans-Atlantic Slave Trade and Slavery*,
United Nations report, April 2021

Mediterranean/Sephardic Jewish Losses

Jews lived for centuries in Spain in relative stability, building a culture highly influenced by their Muslim neighbors. Then new rulers decreed that Jews must either convert to Catholicism or leave in the late 15th Century CE. Before the final expulsion, many were tortured and killed; some left and died or were killed en route; some reached an intended destination but found only temporary safety. The result was near complete destruction of Sephardic Jewish culture and people.

European/Ashkenazi Jewish Losses

After centuries of Polish Jewish culture, there were 3.3 million Jews in Poland before World War II.

Only 380,000 survived, while 2.7 million Polish Jews were murdered...

...Another 1.8 million ethnic Poles were murdered – 10% of the population – as well as many Roma, queers, and others. Poland lost more people to the Holocaust than any other area, including 90% of its Jews. Two-thirds of Europe's Jews, mostly Ashkenazi, were killed.

**These few facts are just meant to turn attention,
for a few moments,
to the depth of loss and grief that we carry,
some of us more than others,
and that we bring into any cross-community dialogue.**

**Of course, these few facts barely scratch the surface
of that depth
and leave whole areas of loss
– and losses of entire communities --
as yet untouched.**

Shrewd Dealings and Dread

Hurston's Moses, still living in the palace, argues with court officials and army officers about the position of *Yisrael-ites*:

> ...they were enemies certainly, because they were treated as such...It was a weak spot in any nation to have a large body of disaffected people within its confines. And then again, civilization and decency demanded less harsh treatment for human beings. If they could not vote and bear arms at once, then shorten their hours of work and repeal the law that said their boy babies must be killed. It was not being obeyed anyway, and since it put [*Mitzrayim*] in a bad light before other nations, why not strike it from the books?
> -- Zora Neale Hurston, *Moses, Man of the Mountain*, -- p.60

The "anti-Hebrew party" dismisses his proposals, but Pharaoh rescinds the order on baby boys and shortens the work day. Moses keeps trying:

> "To outside nations, Pharaoh, we seem better than we are. My idea is, if we wish to be really great is to be better than we seem."

> "Don't be too brash, Moses. I have been thinking too. But it is hard to go against public opinion. The Hebrews are thoroughly hated in [*Mitzrayim*]. I don't say that I did not intensify the feeling to a degree when I came to the throne. But I only played on the instrument I found already. Be patient and some further changes might be declared on my death."

> "Let us hope that might be a long time off. In the meantime their misery is awful. It is too terrible to look at. Go see for yourself."

> "I am old and sick and a trip like that would have me flat on my back for months. I don't believe the country in general would want my days shortened for the sake of those people. They brought it all on themselves anyway. Now, let's table that subject...." -- p.61-62

The the calculations of power and banality of evil are difficult parts of the Exodus story, and of ours.

Pharaoh "Adread," Part 1

The new ruler "did not know Joseph" and placed new burdens on the *Yisrael-ites*. They keep increasing and spreading out, however, and so Pharaoh and his people *va-yakutzu*, which Old JPS translates as "were adread" (Ex 1:12).

This is a serious reaction. In addition to the old-fashioned, but poetically apt, "adread," the Hebrew root kutz [קוץ] can mean "to be grieved, loathe, abhor." Some other (mostly Christian) translations of this verse use the following: loathed, greatly abhorred, came to dread, were grieved, were vexed by, were distressed by, couldn't stand them, feared them worse than before.

So, again, this *kutz*ing is a strong reaction. And it's an important part of how the story develops. It's also an important concept in the way power dynamics work in DC and other places. It's worth some reflection.

This is an important question to consider in a national as well as a local context. And it is central to understanding the intersecting functions of racism and anti-Jewishness. (More on the latter to come).

In the Exodus tale, growing "dread" on the part of *Mitzrayim-ites* contributes to harsher treatment of the *Yisrael-ites,* and finally to attempted genocide. In the U.S., policies and personal behavior fueled by White Supremacy have long contributed to a range of harsh treatment of people seen as non-white: from neighborhood disinvestment, economic and cultural displacement, to outright genocidal actions toward indigenous, Black and brown people.

Moreover, while losing a favorite take-out restaurant or local hangout may seem a far cry from the harsh conditions of the Exodus story, these are not far removed from racist "dread" at all.

Race and Dread

According to a 2019 study by the National Community Reinvestment Coalition, the District of Columbia lost 20,000 Black residents to economic displacement in the study period, 2000-2013. In addition, neighborhoods that were once majority Black are no longer so. Comparing 2000 and 2020 Census data shows that DC lost 80,000 Black people in the two decades. This has many deleterious effects for all, but dangerous effects for remaining Black people in particular.

We see, for example, an increase in precarious incidents involving police in recent years: Police called on a young Black man who was texting someone while waiting his turn at the ATM, in his own neighborhood, which is becoming much whiter and wealthier than it once was. Police called on Black people entering their residences or visiting others, for noise complaints, etc...

As what was once "Chocolate City" continues to attract new residents who "did not know Joseph," conflicts over music/noise are only the tip of the iceberg.

Poverty and Dread

Another example of "hatred always there just below the surface, waiting for the opportunity to arise" involves poverty and housing instability. This overlaps with racist dread -- and we frequently see expressions like "housing voucher holder" used as racist code. This topic will be explored further in the context of Land Use. It's important to note in this context how homeless individuals are stigmatized, suspected of various forms of criminality, and too often blamed for crime and violence in ways that unjustly endanger all unhoused people.

The Talmud (B. Sotah 11a) records a brief disagreement between two rabbis about interpreting Ex 1:8: 1) One said that Pharaoh was really new; and 2) the other said that his decrees were made new....he behaved like one who did not know Joseph at all.

Which leads to these questions:

1) How much can a new ruler change?

2) How much are new rulings the product of other forces -- public opinion, advisors, economic pressures, etc.?

Deal Shrewdly with It

Once the ruler "did not know Joseph," there are worries about how many and how strong the *Yisrael-ite* population is becoming:

> [Pharaoh] said to his people, "Look, the [*Yisrael-ite*] people are more numerous and stronger than we. Come let us deal shrewdly with them, so that they do not increase; otherwise, in event of a war, they might join our enemies in fighting against us and rise up from the ground. -- Ex 1:9-10

הָבָה נִתְחַכְּמָה, לוֹ

Come on, let us deal wisely (King James, 1611)
Come, let us deal shrewdly (JPS 1917 and 1985)
Come, let us outsmart it (Artscroll, 1993)
Come, let us be shrewd with them (Alter, 2004)
Come-now, let us use-our-wits against it (Fox, 1995)

The root of the verb is "wisdom," in this form: "to to show oneself wise, deceive, show one's wisdom." "It" (or "he") is a singular pronoun, referencing the collective "people," sometimes translated as "them."

From its very start, what is now the USA operated so as to "deal shrewdly with" indigenous populations, Africans dragged here and enslaved, and, later, immigrant communities treated with restrictions and suspicion even while welcomed -- or at least permitted -- in for their labor.

U.S. policy and practice in education, employment, courts, housing, health care, and other areas all acted, throughout history, to keep some populations down. Regardless of intent, results for Black communities in particular look remarkably like a successful attempt to "deal shrewdly with them."

This subject is too large to tackle in any serious way here. We can, however, look briefly at U.S. treatment of Black people from the lens of these Exodus verses.

"They Might Join Forces"

To start, **we can look** at who has been easily, legally armed in U.S. history and who has not:

- questions about who should be armed in the Revolutionary War,

- slave patrols and issues of arms in the U.S. Civil War,

- up through current arguments about legal gun ownership

We can look at the words of Glen Ford (1949-2021, z"l), journalist and co-founder of the Black Agenda Report, as well as a soldier during the Viet Nam War. His description of the U.S. military in the late 1960s strongly resembles our passage at the start of Exodus: After seeing Black soldiers unwilling to behave as occupiers at home, the U.S. began militarizing local police instead and shifted the composition of its elite divisions, from majority to Black (in 1968) to predominantly white (today).

The motivating fear here, as Ford tells it, seems quite similar to Pharaoh's: "...young Black men with guns who refused to be counterinsurgency killers either at home or abroad. That would just not do...." (more below).

We can listen to mid-20th Century fear of uprising as a white talk show host demands to know, "whether the Muslim movement [Nation of Islam] does hate me or not and whether it proposes to use force to satisfy its hatred." We can hear historian and political advisor Eric F. Goldman, then moderator of "Open Mind," get increasingly riled at lack of "straight answer," while Baldwin repeatedly notes denial of Black people's humanity and Malcolm X likens the U.S. to Pharaoh, requiring a "complete separation of slave from his slave master."

"Black Muslims in America," NBC-TV's "Open Mind," 4/23/61.
Eric F. Goldman (moderator from 1959-1967) in discussion with:
– author James Baldwin (z"l);
– C. Eric Lincoln, author of *The Black Muslims in America* (1961);
– George Schuyler, editor of *Pittsburgh Courier*; and
– Malcolm X, then Nation of Islam leader.

Malcolm X speeches and interviews collection [sound recordings] 1960-1964 (18 hours of audio). Schomburg Center for Research in Black Culture, New York Public Library.

Video of this show is also widely available on other free platforms.

We can listen to Angela Y. Davis, shortly after her acquittal in the Soledad Brothers Trial:

> The prison system is a weapon of repression. The government views young black and brown people as actually and potentially the most rebellious elements of this society. And thus the jails and prisons of this society are over- flowing with young people of color. Anyone who has seen the streets of ghettos and barrios can already understand how easily a sister or a brother can fall victim to the police who are always there en masse.
> -- 6/9/72 speech delivered at Embassy Auditorium, Los Angeles, IN *Say It Loud*

And recall what the New York Times said at the time of her capture by the FBI:

> ...one who might have made a significant contribution to the nation's normal political debate and to its needed processes of peaceful change became so alienated that she finally went over to revolutionary words and perhaps even worse.
> -- "The Tragedy of Angela Davis," NYT editorial, 10/16/70

It is worth noting that the topics running through this section -- violence, guns, police, etc. -- were among the most challenging for our Cross River Dialogue. Our experiences and opinions ranged as widely as those of Davis and NYT in the early '70s as quoted above. As much as we learned from our dialogue, we had barely began to explore our differences in background, assumptions, and privileges around these topics.... with some of us viewing "event of a war" at home as a distant possibility, while others experience some aspects of community survival as a daily battle and have long been at war.

We'll return to this topic.

----

from **"No Compromise, No Retreat
in the Fight to End Militarism and War,"**
Glen Ford's Keynote Address,
Black Alliance for Peace, April 4, 2019

On the day before that cataclysmic event on April 4, 1968, I was a young a paratrooper with the 82nd Airborne Division. I was out in the field doing exercises with my unit...in Fort Bragg, NC. My unit's duty on that day was to guard the division's headquarters, tents. All that Wednesday, company commanders and executive officers filed into those tents, and they were studying maps of Washington DC so that indeed the division would know how to deploy its troops if we had to occupy the cities in case of an insurrection. The very next day on Thursday, Dr. King was killed and were [sent] into Washington to pacify the city.

That city was burning as were 100 other cities....I didn't know what the commanding officers thought their mission was, but the Black soldiers of the 82nd Airborne Division knew what our assignment had to be. As far as we were concerned our mission came from Dr. King and from Malcolm....

At that time the 82nd Airborne Division was 60% Black, and the Black troops on that day were united in the mission of ensuring that the white soldiers didn't harm one head in Washington, DC. [All were aware of what had happened in Newark NJ the year before, when National Guardsmen killed 26 men, women, and children.] The Black troops of the 82nd Airborne Division swore that the racist occupation of Newark would not be repeated on our watch, not in DC after they had killed Dr. King. And nobody was harmed by the occupying 82nd because the Black soldiers would not stand for it.

And that is not just an anecdote, brothers and sisters. That was the beginning of the end of the draft in the United States: The United States military discovered that it couldn't control a Black ghetto army, that these heavily Black units saw themselves as guardians of the Black population and not as occupiers.

...after 1968, the Joint Chiefs of the United States Armed Forces were already despairing about the usefulness of a draft army that wound up filling elite units, like my 82 Airborne Division, with majorities of Black soldiers, young Black men with guns who refused to be counterinsurgency killers either at home or abroad. That would just not do....

The antiwar movement of that era thinks that they defeated the draft, and certainly the civilian mass movement was a big factor in getting rid of mass conscription. But after 1968, the Joint Chiefs of the United States Armed Forces were already despairing about the usefulness of a draft army that wound up filling elite units, like my 82nd Airborne Division, with majorities of Black soldiers. Young Black men with guns who refused to be counter-insurgency killers either at home or abroad -- that would just not do. They had to make that change.

If you try to reinstate the draft today, it would be the top military brass that would be the most vocal opponents of the draft. They love the all-volunteer army. Ashton Carter, who was Obama's Defense Secretary, said they loved the all-volunteer military because they get to pick who serves in it.

And today, my old paratrooper unit -- the 82nd, which was 60% Black back in 1968 -- is the whitest unit in the whole US Army. That is by design.

Blacks still make up a disproportionate share of the Army, about 20%, but they're clustered in support units -- driving trucks, supply units, things like that...Super elite troops of the Special Operations Command are overwhelmingly white, and that is by design....
 -- full recording at Facebook page for Black Alliance for Peace,
 excerpt used with permission of the author, $z''/$

Adding Enemies, Part 1

Some commentaries on Ex 1:10, focus on political strategy involved in the phrase translated as "deal shrewdly" -- or "use-our-wits against it" or "outsmart it" or "deal wisely." Based, no doubt on circumstances of their authors, a number explain why Pharaoh did not want to directly confront the

> ### "...add enemies..." (Ex 1:10)
>
> *Nosaf*/add resonates with Joseph [*Yosef*], a name given by his mother Rachel to mean "May God add for me another son" (Gen 30:24).
>
> Everett Fox translates to closely mimic the Hebrew:
>
> > Come-now, let us use-our-wits against it,
> > lest it become many-more,
> > and then, if war should occur,
> > it too be added to our enemies
> > and make was upon us
> > or go up away from the land!
> > – Ex 1:10, Fox, *Five Books of Moses*

Yisrael-ites and show the ruler considering how to be rid of the *Yisrael-ites* without actually expelling them:

1) Sforno (c.1470-1550 CE, Italy) describes Pharaoh's thought process this way: If we do not have adequate reason to expel them we would become pariahs among our neighbors.

2) Ramban (1194-1270 CE, Spain) says that "deal shrewdly" means imposing taxes on foreigners, a common practice in biblical times and his own. Such a course of action, Pharaoh argues in this scenario, would not appear to "be acting out of hate" but would eventually achieve the goal.

2) *Tur HaArokh* (c.1280-c.1340, Germany & Spain) says Pharaoh was afraid an order to destroy the *Yisrael-ites* would not be obeyed. He says descendants of Joseph's sons, Ephraim and Menashe, who "possessed considerable influence in the highest government circles, and the very number of *Yisrael-ites* would make open warfare, which they would surely resist a highly dangerous undertaking.

> ### History Note:
>
> From the 1490s through early decades of the 16th Century CE, Jews who had been expelled from Spain took up residence in what is now known as Italy. In the mid-16th Century, however, shortly after Sforno's time, Jews were expelled from Naples and some other areas of Italy as well.
>
> Meanwhile, across Europe for centuries, Jews and other minorities were taxed as a condition of living as "strangers to the realm." Such taxes rose and fell, depending on economic conditions and goals of those in power.

For much of U.S. history, segregation was legal, as were housing covenants which affected both Jews and Blacks in DC (more later). Local and national leaders were long applauded, rather than thought to be pariahs, for keeping Black people away from some areas to live, work, attend school, or otherwise participate in community life.

Later, when segregation was no longer strictly legal, Pharaoh-like "shrewdness," including a huge variety of "taxes" on Black people were adopted as a way of effecting expulsion without appearing to have that aim...or, at least, while maintaining plausible deniability about the aim. As touched on already, tens of thousands of Black people have been displaced from DC, in the past 20 years, due to what are sometimes called -- with a view to plausible deniability -- "market forces." (More on this to come.)

Other, related parts of Pharaoh's deliberations, according to Sforno and others, were issues of "cultural incompatibility."

Bible verses mentioning regular daily life for *Yisrael-ites* and *Mitzrayim-ites* suggest that the two groups ate different foods, spoke different languages, and maintained separate cultural rituals (possibly, depending on the commentary, including circumcision among *Yisrael-ites* but not *Mitzrayim-ites*). A variety of commentaries has long suggested that Pharaoh found the *Yisrael-ites* dangerous because they remained too culturally distinct -- an interpretation of "too many and too strong."

Pharaoh's objection to *Yisrael-ites* maintaining cultural distinction is sometimes linked to

- a fear that foreign culture would overwhelm *Mitzrayim-ite* culture;

- a fear that remaining culturally distinct would facilitate a *Yisrael-ite* conquest of the land and/or expulsion of the *Mitzrayim-ites;* and

- schemes of Pharaoh to get rid of the *Yisrael-ites* by making aspects of their culture illegal or inconvenient and/or by encouraging assimilation.

Commentary threads around "cultural incompatibility" reflect historical experience -- in many places, across centuries -- for Jews of various ethnic and cultural backgrounds in relationship to the surrounding mainstream culture. Also reflected are arguments among Jews about possibility and advisability of assimilation and about implications of appearing "too many" and "too strong" -- often understood today as "too visible" or "too vocal."

But Jewish communities are not the only ones to grapple with issues of cultural distinction, "incompatibility," and the implications of Pharaoh's fears.

Pharaoh "Adread," Part 2

In addition to issues of race and poverty, Pharaoh and the people "adread" raises the topic of anti-Jewishness -- often: "antisemitism," discussed in the introduction and related to "cultural incompatibility" below.

We saw Pharaoh try to "deal shrewdly with [the *Yisrael-ites*], so that they do not increase" (Ex 1:8-10). When the *Yisrael-ites* keep increasing and spreading out, Pharaoh and his people "were adread [*va-yakutzu*]" (Ex 1:12).

Above, we touched on reflections of this passage in history of the U.S. The same "adread" dynamic also resonates with Jewish history: Poland. England. The Ottoman Empire. Italy. Spain. Parts of Northern Africa and Southwest Asia. So many places over the centuries welcomed, or at least tolerated, Jews as minority communities in the realm... until those same places turned dangerous, if not lethal, to Jews, subjecting them to legal and physical attacks, expulsion, and murder.

This dread, this *kutz*ing, results in death for many and much suffering -- in Exodus and in history. And, in both Exodus and history, it's not immediately clear how not-knowing-Joseph is related to this "adread" reaction. The role Joseph played for the *Mitzrayim* economy, and what it means to not-know that, will be explored in the discussion on land use, ahead. For now, recall that Joseph was well-placed in the administration, second only to Pharaoh of the time. And then consider this analysis:

> ...The oppression of Jews is a conjuring trick, a pressure valve, a shunt that redirects the rage of working people away from the 1%, a hidden mechanism, a set up that works through misdirection, that uses privilege to hide the gears.
>
> Unlike racism, at least some of its targets must be seen to prosper, must be well paid and highly visible. The goal is not to crush us, it's to have us available for crushing. Christian rulers use us to administer their power, to manage for them, and set us up in the window displays of capitalism for the next time the poor pick up stones to throw. What is hard for the angry multitudes to see is that Jews don't succeed in spite of our oppression. We are kept insecure by our history of sudden assaults, and some of us, a minority of us, are offered the uncertain bribes of privilege and protection. Privilege for a visible sample of us is the only way to make the whole tricky business work....
> -- Aurora Levins Morales in *Understanding Antisemitism: An Offering to Our Movement* from Jews for Racial & Economic Justice (JFREJ)

Image: one Venn diagram set of contradictory realities, a detail from JFREJ's "Unraveling Anti-semitism" poster. (More on the poster ahead.) "Antisemitism is dangerous and real" overlaps with "False claims of antisemitism are weaponized by the right."

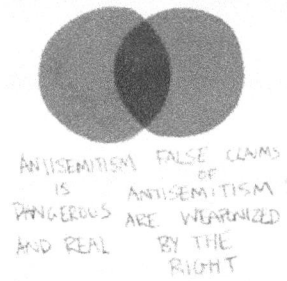

ANTISEMITISM FALSE CLAIMS
IS   OF
DANGEROUS   ANTISEMITISM
AND REAL   ARE WEAPONIZED
                      BY THE
                      RIGHT

Coded Threat

JFREJ does not use biblical comparison in their analysis, quoted in part above. However, the Exodus text provides another way of viewing how "the trick works." And a close look at Pharaoh's words can be helpful in understanding the threat of coded language.

A Talmudic commentary says that Pharaoh knew Joseph and his accomplishments but started to behave as though he did not (Sotah 11a). This is not unlike historical leaders deciding that economic conditions have changed and past alliances with Jews are no longer needed, so making new edicts -- which have, often across history, included oppression and violence against Jews.

Back in the Bible, Pharaoh says, "Behold, the people of the children of Yisrael are too mighty [עָצוּם, atzum] for us." While "*atzum*" means "strong" or "mighty," the word is also linked to "self" or "essence."

Ibn Ezra (12th Century Spain) notes the unusual grammar: "the people, the children of Israel." He says the latter phrase explains the identity of this people, rather than simply naming them.

With these three readings in mind, Ex 1:9 looks like a leader signaling the populace to watch out for "these people -- you know what they're like." (Returning to the passage quoted in part above):

> ...Then, when the wrath of the most oppressed, whether Russian peasants starving on potatoes or urban US People of Color pressed to the wall, reaches boiling point, there we are: The Tsar's tax collector, the shopkeeper and the pawnbroker, the landlord and the lawyer, the social worker and the school administrator. And whether it's a Polish aristocrat watching the torches go by on pogrom or the Episcopalian banker discreetly out of sight while working-class people tell each other that Jews control the economy, the trick works. -- A. Levins Morales/*Understanding Antisemitism*, continued

Many Jews have direct connections, sometimes not long past, with what can happen when a leader tells followers to watch out for "these people."

Others know this threat through more general history. But most grown-up Jews I know have powerful, fear-filled reactions to hearing a contemporary leader or preacher or scholar start talking about how society's problems are due to "these people." Their fears are not unfounded but can seem far-fetched to those who have not learned, or inherited, a reaction to that coded language.

Meanwhile, of course, Jews are not the only ones to know, and fear, "these people" speech.

Part of the Trick

Anti-Jewish oppression is a tool -- a sadly effective one -- for reinforcing unjust systems and promoting divisions among people who might other-wise join together to address the source of our very real problems. As

----

"Unraveling Antisemitism" is described as "a cultural organizing project and map for discussion, organizing, & struggle to win a world free from antisemitism." It is available, along with related curriculum materials, from JFREJ, who spent three years of study and reflection producing it. Their 2017 *Understanding Antisemitism*, quoted above, is also available for free download from their website.

(Image: top portion of Unraveling Anti-semitism poster, a complex graphic filled with drawings, diagrams, and hand-written notes. Visit JFREJ.org for full description and opportunities to obtain a copy and support their work.)

Unraveling Antisemitism includes a series of "contradicting truths," and a number of other elements meant to emphasize that there are multiple per-spectives at any moment and multiple histories leading to that point. Learning to hold contradiction, to accept that there are always multiple valid perspectives, is one of the tools for foiling "the trick."

noted in the quotation above and in many other sources, anti-Jewishness works differently than, but also in conjunction with, racism and other forms of oppression.

It is absolutely crucial to understand that anti-Jewishness works by establishing "privilege for a visible sample of us." A similar-looking dynamic sets some Black (or other oppressed) people as examples of "success," in an attempt to dispel the facts of the oppressive system. But anti-Jewishness relies on the visible privileged in a very specific way. JFREJ's "Unraveling Antisemitism" does an excellent job of illustrating this and many other points about anti-Jewishness and how it works in conjunction with, and to support, other forms of oppression.

A Counter-Trick

Here JFREJ's explanation for the series of "contradicting truths," those two-circle Venn diagrams, like those shared here as examples:

> Bordering the charts about antisemitism and Jews are a series of contradicting assertions we wrestle with when talking about Jews, are a series of contradicting assertions we wrestle with when talking about Jews, antisemitism, and racial capitalism. Each set of statements is illustrated as two overlapping circles, to represent that the two statements can seem opposing, but are both true.
>
> The vents in the piece were made out of translucent plastic. They almost look like stained glass, alluding to the holy and spiritual nature of the work.
> -- from the Unraveling Antisemitism discussion guide

Here are a few pertinent pairs of truths:

> Antisemitism is dangerous and real. False claims of antisemitism are weaponized by the right. (above)

> All Jews are targeted by antisemitism. Being visibly Jewish increases your risk of being targeted by antisemitism.

> Jews of Color experience racism in & out of Jewish community. Jews of color experience antisemitism in & out of community of color.

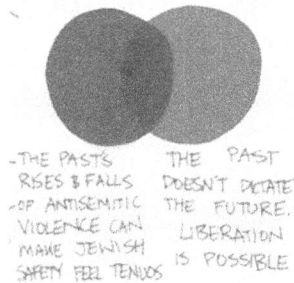

-THE PAST'S RISES & FALLS -OF ANTISEMITIC VIOLENCE CAN MAKE JEWISH SAFETY FEEL TENUOS   THE PAST DOESN'T DICTATE THE FUTURE. LIBERATION IS POSSIBLE

> The past's rises and falls of antisemitic violence can make Jewish safety feel tenuous. The past doesn't dictate the future. Liberation is possible. (shown here)

More practice with multiple perspectives will ultimately make it harder for anyone to pull off the kind of trick that makes anti-Jewishness work. If we see Exodus 1:9 as about

- anti-Black racism AND

- about anti-Jewishness AND

- about the perils of militarism or nationalism AND

- about individual leadership styles AND

- a host of other readings,

there is no place for pitting one group of people against another.

The text then becomes a tool of community- and collaboration-building, rather than one of division.

The experience of Cross River Dialogue shows, if nothing else, the necessity and urgency of this kind of work is, pitfalls and all.

Adding Enemies, Part 2

As we've seen, the *Yisrael-ite* people increase and grow strong, and Pharaoh becomes concerned lest they "may join our enemies" or "add themselves" (Ex 1:10). Concern about how a people within one's borders might act in event of war and broader accusations of "dual loyalty," have long affected Black and Jewish communities in the U.S., and this arose in numerous ways in our Cross River Dialogue.

Jews and non-Jews in the CRD group have been accused of dual loyalty due to solidarity with people of color globally, particularly with Palestinians.

Jews living in many places over the centuries have been accused of dual loyalty, sometimes of sole loyalty, to the Jewish People rather than to the country of residence. For that reason, among others, Jews historically argued amongst ourselves about if/how to support a Jewish homeland. The modern state of Israel brings additional "dual loyalty" complications for Jews and for dialogue that involves Jews.

When CRD started, some wished to entirely avoid questions involving Israel/Palestine in order to focus on bridging local divides. Some cited pan-African concerns as meaning oppression in Palestine and in the U.S. are inseparable. Still others thought we could profitably focus on clarifying differences between "anti-Israel" or "anti-Zionist" positions and "anti-Jewish" ("antisemitic") ones; discussing this could help us deal with ways in which these issues interfere with our work in the wider world. As it happened, those stances didn't change, but the decision about whether and how to discuss issues around Israel, Zionism, and Palestinians was not entirely in our hands....

...Over the course of our time together, and with our group never larger than twelve people, CRD saw a number of incidents in which someone connected to one or more of us, personally and/or as part of an organization, was under fire for perceived anti-Jewishness. In addition to the kerfuffle that helped launch the dialogue group, one or more of us was in some way linked to the following people when they were attacked for supposed anti-Jewishness:

Marc Lamont Hill,
Ilhan Omar,
Bernie Sanders,
Angela Davis,
Tamika Mallory,
Linda Sarsour,
the entire Women's March of 2020, and
Dr. Natalie Hopkinson of Don't Mute DC

-- and that's just in the span of about 30 months....

Anti-Jewishness and its weaponization, particularly as a charge against Black people, is an on-going issue -- nationally and locally -- and was a difficult area for Cross River Dialogue.

In addition, CRD spent substantial time discussing or responding to specific initiatives of our local government. The two most prominent issues were our local police training with Israel Defense Forces and a proposed public-private partnership with DC's Office of Human Rights called "Jews and Allies United." Either one of these initiatives could launch whole bookshelves of discussion on their own. They also return the spotlight to the topic of "dual loyalty" and questions about who is read as "enemies" and who is read as "us" in Ex. 1:10.

Although much of the discussion in this book is challenging,
the next three pages in particular touch on potentially triggering material.

Some of what follows is personal reflection -- and mostly about process.

Included is an essay already published by some CRD participants.

Material below does not include details of physical violence of 8/11/2017.
But it does discuss violent dynamics setting Jewish concerns apart
from those of other, intersecting communities at risk from neo-Nazis.

Please read on if able. OR skip ahead to "Topic for Another Time."

Rereading4Liberation.com

"Enemy" vs "Us"

Backstory but no Precedent. CRD's first, exploratory gathering was in July 2018, just weeks before "Unite the Right II" was scheduled to arrive in Washington, DC, on the first anniversary of events in Charlottesville, VA, that led, among other horrors, to the killing of Heather Heyer.

Our first meeting exemplified many of the challenges of cross-community dialogue already touched on here: We came together from unequal positions in terms of everyday sense of safety. We brought vastly different experiences, or lack thereof, of physical danger and of risk, whether chosen or not. We showed up with huge differences in assumptions about so many aspects of the world -- most pertinent here, what can safely be ignored and what must be addressed directly.

Meanwhile, the brand new CRD had no precedent or established protocols. So, figuring out if/how to respond to anything at all was not simple. Talk of Nazis coming to town was raising alarm bells for participants, more confusing than compelling. And, while we were trying to respond, I suspect that those of us who were not in Charlottesville in 2017 did not grok the trauma of those events and what the anniversary was raising. Moreover, our little group was meeting in the long, related shadow of the prior year's struggle around the March for Racial Justice, the anniversary of the Elaine Massacre, and Yom Kippur. No decisions were made.

Institutional Action. A few weeks later (Aug 6), the Anti-Defamation League (ADL) and Jewish Community Relations Council (JCRC) of Greater Washington issued a joint "Community Advisory," unsurprisingly focused on Jewish concerns:

> August 12th marks the one-year anniversary of the *Unite the Right* rally in Charlottesville, Virginia, the largest and most violent gathering of white supremacists in decades. Like you, we remain deeply disturbed and impacted by this event and by the actions of those who felt emboldened to march with torches across the University of Virginia campus shouting "sieg heil!" and "Jews will not replace us!"
>
> For many, Charlottesville delivered a wake-up call-showing us just how deadly the current rise in bigotry, racism, and anti-Semitism can be. This year's anniversary is a painful reminder that hatred is still alive and well in our country, and that we must stand together and draw strength from our diversity in order to fight against it.

The bulk of the statement discussed security issues and cooperation with law enforcement, suggestions for "alternative unity-focused programs," and not one word about the Stop the Hate coalition that had been months in the making. Shortly after the statement was issued, many Jewish groups and congregations in the area began encouraging members to "stay away."

On the Record. After much discussion between individuals within CRD, conscious that the monthly meeting schedule -- of this brand new group -- would not permit collective response, several of CRD's Jewish participants, with help from a few other Jews, together crafted a statement that was published on the *Forward*'s "Scribe" platform, August 10, 2018.

Substantial excerpts are included here (full piece is still on Scribe) to share some of the ways a number of us, Jews and non-Jews, felt abandoned in very dangerous ways by the loudest voices of the Jewish establishment.

"On The Anniversary Of Charlottesville, Don't Forget That Nazis Hate More Than Just Jews"

[The ADL/JCRC advisory of August 6] speaks of "the current rise in bigotry, racism, and anti-Semitism" and says "we must stand together and draw strength from our diversity in order to fight against it." There is no indication, however, that ADL and JCRC are standing with — or even communicating with — the diverse coalition that has been working for months to engage together in the very fight ADL and JCRC say must be waged. In fact, the advisory mentions no contact with non-Jewish communities, in the District and beyond, for whom the "Unite the Right II" rally is life-threatening.

...I was disturbed to see that the Metropolitan Police Department is the only local institution mentioned in the advisory....I am worried to see ADL and JCRC announce that they are "tracking the situation" involving counter-protesters, as though community and advocacy groups I support are part of the threat. [In addition: None of the "alternative unity-focused programs" included any non-Jews from threatened communities, and all were located in whiter and wealthier areas of the region.]

It is not unusual for national organizations...to treat the District as a national entity, not a city with its own culture and concerns....Still, it is disconcerting to see ADL and JCRC largely ignore the local context.

Meanwhile, in another August 6 statement, Truah: the Rabbinic Call for Human Rights addresses the upcoming anniversary without mentioning Washington, DC at all....Truah declares its support for Charlottesville's refusal to permit this year's White Supremacist rally. But they ignore the fact that a federal agency granted the permit they are applauding Charlottesville for refusing.

Truah "will be in Charlottesville again this year, standing with them and other minority communities and communities of color targeted by white supremacist words and deeds," their August 6 statement reads. But my town, where the anniversary White Supremacist rally is actually scheduled to take place, is not even mentioned.

....Bend the Arc, #WeveSeenThisBefore notwithstanding, has been entirely silent on the Charlottesville anniversary....

The approach to August 11-12 has been an opportunity for Jews and other communities attacked by White Supremacists to join together. Some Jewish organizations, including local chapters of Jewish Voice for Peace and If Not Now, have joined the Shut It Down DC coalition in solidarity with Black, indigenous, Muslim, LGBTQ+, Latinx, Asian, disabled and many other DC communities. Mainstream Jewish institutions like JCRC and ADL, however, have failed the call....

....It's important to note, as an example for Jews everywhere to ponder, that the DC area "Community Advisory" declares that ADL and JCRC are working closely with local police, encourages institutions to review their security procedures, and asks people to notify the police if "anyone acts in a threatening or suspicious manner or uses violence."

...Truah, some local Jewish organizations and individual Jews have likewise stood in solidarity with Black Lives Matter. But how many consider what it might mean, especially for black and brown neighbors — including members of Jewish communities — to then rely on police protection if "anyone acts in a threatening or suspicious manner"?

Rosh Hodesh Elul, when Jews worldwide listen to the sound of the shofar calling them to reflection and a better new year, begins on August 12. Perhaps we have missed some opportunities to unite with non-Jewish neighbors in opposing White Supremacy in our midst. But there is still time to consider what kind of neighbors we will be in 5779.

Virginia A. Spatz, in collaboration with Scott Brown, Chase Carter, Sig Cohen, Rachel Usdan, and other members of DC's Cross River (Black-Jewish) Dialogue.

Topic for Another Time

There is much more to consider and discuss here in an effort to build better cross-community dialogue and collaboration in the future. Perhaps at some point, we can gather reflections from those involved in the Cross River Dialogue and in some of the backstory events. What happened with Jewish involvement in the March for Racial Justice (2017) and then the Stop the Hate rally (2018) is an unhealed wound. Just one of many such that will continue to effect dialogue across our intersecting Black and Jewish communities...unless and until we figure out how to address the harm.

Trust and Respect

As mentioned briefly earlier, the entire period of the Counting is considered one of semi-mourning by many Jews. Music, dancing, weddings, and many forms of pleasure are avoided during these weeks -- with a shift in custom, beginning on the 33rd Day, which is called "*Lag B'omer.*"

"*Lag*" is just the number 33 in Hebrew. And there is a tradition that mourning is lifted, either temporarily -- just on the 33rd day -- or for the remainder of the seven weeks.

One explanation for mourning in this period is linked to an important figure in Jewish tradition: Rabbi Akiva is identified with the time between destruction of the Temple (70 CE) and the Bar Kochba Rebellion (132 CE). The story goes that in R' Akiva's study house a plague arose, killing 12,000 pairs of students or 24,000 total. The plague ended on *Lag B'omer.*

The deaths are attributed in the Talmud to "lack of respect" (Babylonian Talmud Yevamot 62b).

So, *Lag B'omer* seems a good time to focus on respect.

Some commentary focuses on the **pairs** of students who died. Studying with a partner is crucial in Jewish tradition, and these partnerships are important relationships. So, attributing the plague to disrespect is making a strong statement about how the pairs filed one another. Also, some wonder: How could the head of a study house, who is ultimately responsible for all these students, miss all this strife under his nose? The conclusion: The students were outwardly engaging in discussion, apparently learning from one another, while harboring disrespect in their hearts.

...For those keeping score in Hebrew: There are 32 days of plague and 17 days afterward. This is equivalent to the Hebrew words "*lev tov* [good heart]" — *lamed* + *bet* (32) and *tet* + *vav* + *bet* (17). So, the teaching suggests that the "good heart" seems to have been missing from Akiva's study house.

Bringing the topic back to intergroup dialogue today: Can cross-community dialogue help illuminate areas where there is an erroneous impression that "all is well" while community members harbors disrespect? What other tools do we have?

Modeling Respect

More on the same Rabbi Akiva and all those pairs of students lost:

> ...While living apart from his wife for all of those years [to facilitate his teaching, he lived in Jerusalem; his wife remained at home], Rabbi Akiva did not show his students the daily habits of respect. How were his students to learn how to treat each other with respect if Rabbi Akiva did not model this for them? This is reminiscent of the adage, "Tell me and I forget, show me and I remember, involve me and I understand." On Lag B'Omer we should take a moment and try to learn the lesson that evaded Rabbi Akiva's students. How should treat each other with respect? It is clearly not enough to just talk about it. If we want to teach respect we need to model it.

> How are we any different from the students of Rabbi Akiva? How can we in the religious establishment hope to teach people about respect when we do not model it ourselves? Not modeling basic human respect seems to be a true abomination.

> ...It is not enough just to talk about, or even just to show respect; we need to find new ways to involve each other in building respectful communities. So soon, with Lag B'Omer behind us, we can all get married.
> -- Rabbi Avi Orlow, "Modeling Respect on Lag B'Omer" on behalf of Keshet: For LGBTQ Equality in Jewish Life, 4/19/2013 (Whole piece on My Jewish Learning)

This piece was written during a year that proved to be a big one, legally, for gay marriage in the U.S. The current events topic involves Orthodox Jews and same-sex marriage, which is not directly relevant to *Rereading Exodus along the Anacostia*. But the overall lesson is one that applies: The need to model respect as well to "talk about it," with the aim of "building respectful communities."

Intergroup Dialogue and Respect

A few years ago, a shooting occurred around the corner from the author's house, resulting in neighborhood calls for more police. Rather than involve the entire CRD, two of us -- myself and one non-Jewish Black participant, Maurice Cook -- together wrote to the local paper, *Hill Rag* ("Don't Over Police Hill East" June 2019):

> We are experiencing an escalation of Anti-Black expression in Hill East from residents expecting a level of safety and comfort that has been unavailable to longtime residents over the last 35 years. The result, if the course is not changed before it's too late, will be trau-

matizing, if not lethal, to Black residents and ineffective in creating better community for anyone.

Research shows that the U.S. population, Black and not, is susceptible to anti-Black bias which is reinforced in countless ways every day. Additional research shows that police training, however inadvertently, promotes associations between "black" and "criminal"...

The two of us are members of DC's Cross River Dialogue...We are learning together that fear and lack of contact between communities too often breeds objectification and danger and even calls for extermination. So we applaud [a community leader's] suggestion to get neighbors together, for a street party or other communal activity, as a response to the growing unrest. But we equally believe that Black residents of, and visitors to, [the area] must never be expected to prove their innocence or worth, to other neighbors or to police.

...CRD recognizes that real safety can only be built through trust and trust can only be built by truly being in relationship with one another. We, CRD members and long-time residents of what is now "Hill East," call on all our neighbors to work toward true relationship and to consider the costs to our neighborhood as a whole and to our Black neighbors in particular, of increased police presence.

This was written less than three years ago, but I am not sure I would write it today: Is the, or even a, problem lack of contact? lack of true relationship?

With each passing year, I despair of reaching a point where no neighbor's innocence or worth are up for debate. I have less and less confidence that we will ever learn to discuss safety in an inclusive and life-affirming way.

I still know that we are obligated to try, however. And it is hoped that these questions we are exploring will help us find new ways forward.... Here, to close out this section is a perhaps related story.

I've heard versions of the following story told at the Jewish high holidays, when we are focusing on repentance and "return." I don't know it's origin, and I'm guessing there are versions from many traditions.

In any case, here it is:

Two individuals meet in the woods. Both are lost. They have the following exchange:

"Friend, I am lost, can you tell me the way out?"

"I cannot tell you the way, for am lost, too. But I **can** tell you that the way I came does not lead out of here."
[Some add:] "Perhaps we can look together."

War and Land

Moses tried -- in the scene from *Moses, Man of the Mountain*, previously quoted -- to turn Pharaoh's attention to needs of his country rather than making war with foreign powers. At the close of what proves their last conversation while Moses is still under Pharaoh's roof, Pharaoh insists that Mitzrayim doesn't "have any home problems that I can see" -- *Moses*, p.62

And that's the end of the matter for Pharaoh.

This short scene captures a key challenge in developing trust and respect, as raised in the last section, particularly amid threat of enemies and war.

As previously noted, one of Pharaoh's stated fears at the start of Exodus is that the *Yisrael-ites* will "join enemies...in the event of a war" (Ex 1:10). But one of the themes that we see in the Bible's Exodus, in Hurston's work, and in U.S. history alike is that not everyone agrees when a war has started -- and thus, who has reason to be suspicious of whom.

For example, return to Angela Davis, quoted in "Let us Deal Shrewdly," declaring in 1972 "how easily a sister or a brother can fall victim to the police who are always there en masse," while the New York Times speaks as though there had been peace before she "went over to revolutionary words and perhaps even worse."

Or return to the question of where a story starts: with a police officer's decision to act in a way that ends an individual's life or with one or more of the precipitating conditions.

As we move into issues of land use, it is worthwhile to remain mindful of how housing reflects and interacts with many aspects of basic survival.... and how some of us have long been at war while others "don't have any home problems that I can see."

35

"If You Lived Here"

As discussed previously, deciding where a story starts is crucial to the shape of the tale and meaning-making around it. Popular versions of the Exodus narrative, including Hurston's *Moses* and the movies, *The Prince of Egypt* and *The Ten Commandments*, begin with the *Yisrael-ites* already living in *Mitzrayim*. But the Book of Exodus itself begins with Jacob's extended clan traveling to *Mitzrayim* (and Joseph "already there"). In most Passover tellings, the story also begins with ancestors of the *Yisrael-ites*.

For this Stage, we back up to consider the story of how the *Yisrael-ites* come to be found in *Mitzrayim*. To begin: imagine a realtor selling high-end dwellings in the city of Pitom, where enslaved people were forced to build storage facilities (Ex 1:11). Then take a look at the DC-area public television program, "If You Lived Here," launched during the pandemic (2021).

The first episodes of the new series are case studies in residential displacement, gentrification through erasing existing local commerce, and the consequences of promoting density as a solution to for increased affordability of housing.

"H Street Corridor"

The first episode, "H Street Corridor," is an illustration, however unintentional, of everything Brandi Thompson Summers writes in her insightful 2019 book, *Black in Place: The Spatial Aesthetics of Race in a Post-Chocolate City*. In short, professor Summers uses H Street NE to explain how "blackness has become a prized and lucrative aesthetic that often leaves out D.C.'s Black residents."

WETA's "H Street Corridor" advertises the area's Black history while simultaneously promoting "cranes in the sky at all times" and other evidence of displacement. We're told, for example, that what was once a single-family home was converted to two units, each selling for $775,000, "because of the cost of dirt" in the neighborhood.

One interviewee describes Maketto Market, in the 1300 block of H Street, as "an homage to the H Street of old." As part of a "revitalization" narrative, we are told that, "for a 30- or 40-year period, this was not so much of a destination." Thus: $28 fried chicken and $33 "cool kids vinyl" in the former Dollar Store space, in the block which once housed French's Fine Southern Cuisine and Ohio Restaurant: Southern Style Home Cooking. Later, a realtor casually references "a really cool church converted to condos" down the block from a $2.5 million home, pointing to, but not naming, the former Imani Temple African-American Catholic Congregation.

Selling the City

Douglas Development is one of the largest developers in DC, the largest for commercial real estate (according to *Washington Business Journal* in 2021). Douglas owns property along H Street Northeast: commercial buildings at 1236, 1344-46, 1360, and 1378 H Street NE, and a mixed-use development at 501 H NE.

To sell potential tenants on the eastern end of the H Street corridor, the developer cites proximity to Union Station at the western end of the corridor, with "easy access to the metropolitan area and the East Coast." In addition, they declare a "renaissance" led by "a hip arts scene, inclusive of quirky bars, eclectic restaurants, art galleries, and regional music destinations–most locally owned."

A slightly fresher-looking listing, for 1236 H, offers a "Booming Entertainment District."

The description used for 1360 and 1378 H NE seems about five years out-of-date: Mosaic Theater Company, which launched at Atlas Theater – across the street -- in fall 2015, is missing. And the photo for 1378 H shows Ohio Restaurant, which -- although it dominated the corner for decades, long after it was closed -- was replaced by Turning Natural in 2016. (The Douglas Development webpage for 1344-46 contains nothing but a photo and contact information.)

Screen-shot from Douglas Development webpage showing Rose DeJavu, which was located at 1378 but closed during the pandemic. (Fuller image description p.134)

In a flyer advertising 501 H Street NE, Douglas describes H Street as follows:

"1000+ new residential units delivered in 2016 within a half mile"

"A new 38,000 SF Whole Foods opened in March of 2017"

"72% of residents within a 1/2 mile have a Bachelor's Degree or higher"

THE H STREET VIBE is unlike any other in the District. Unique and authentic, this is where the residents of Washington DC live, work, and celebrate. Here, a vibrant collection of shops, bars, restaurants, and retailers serves a residential base that has experienced – and continues to experience enormous growth as H Street transforms into one of DC's most happening corridors.

No people appear in visuals for the four eastern properties, but they do promise "hip." The flyer for 501 H (image below) includes only white people. This is not un-common for Douglas. They are selling "unique and authentic," but not necessarily to or for those who provide that "authenticity" -- what professor Summers calls that "prized and lucrative aesthetic that often leaves out D.C.'s Black residents."

Flyer from Douglas website for 501 H St, NE shows mosaic of four photos: whole building, bike racks, and street-level retail -- all with no people visible -- then four white people seated together at an outdoor table. (Fuller description p.134)

Another example of what and how Douglas sells is 1500 North Capitol, northwest of H Street and at the edge of Shaw.

(Leasing flyer. Image description p.134.)

If Who Lived Here?

Before moving toward the Shaw episode of "If You Lived Here," return for a moment to those high-end dwellings in Pitom. A tale of housing already for sale is one story, with an obvious starting place. But who convinced potential residents that the area was "hip"? How do long-time residents and formerly-enslaved people fit into the story of the new, hip Pitom? And what kind of stories about the not-so-hip, old Pitom helped pave the way for the new?

Also: How long did developers let properties sit, waiting for the day they could cash in, instead of contributing to the vibrancy of Pitom all along?

Grit: for only $2.5 million

The "Shaw" episode, number 2 in the "If You Lived Here" series, highlights a Black past and a "diverse" area, but fails to mention Shaw's enormous population shift, between 2000 and 2016: a substantial decline in Black residents, in lower income residents, and in families with children, as well as a large increase in white residents, middle-high income residents, and residents aged 18-34.

Shaw is advertised as a place that "has grit" as a sales frame for 2- and 3-bedroom homes with purchase prices of between $829,000 and $2.5 million. There is no mention of the "Don't Mute DC" movement, launched (see above) around the corner from the spotlighted luxury homes.

On an ironic "where are the copy editors?!" note: A musical history segment tells us that Marvin Gaye (1939-1984) was "from Southeast." In actuality, he was born at Freedman's Hospital in Northwest, lived his earliest years in Southwest, and is best known for connections to Simple City (Northeast), meaning that Southeast is the one quadrant with which Marvin Gaye is **not** associated.

The "If You Lived Here"series "spotlights a wide array of neighborhoods and properties throughout the national capital area while celebrating each area's history, culture, notable places and flavor." The "flavor" presented in the H Street and Shaw episodes is served up as part of a package that can be purchased, rather than as an element of community in which to participate. Neighborhoods are laid out as commodities on offer, for a hefty price, rather as than as dynamic systems in which newcomers should expect to contribute.

Disparity and Displacement

Geographical Note: Rock Creek and the park surrounding it form a geographic feature in DC's northwest used for more than a century for segregationist purposes, some formal and legal and some informal.

The Anacostia River, to the east, has also been a severe demographic divider for decades.

Both are also lovely natural resources apart from politics.

DC has lived with decades of income disparity linked with de facto segregation, as described in this DC Policy Center report:

> Between 2000 and 2017, the most notable change in the maps is that, as most of D.C. between Rock Creek and the Anacostia gentrified, the region's poorest neighborhoods almost all became concentrated east of the Anacostia River.
> -- D.W. Rowlands,

"How household incomes in the D.C. area have changed since 1980"

The District experienced more gentrification than any other city in the U.S., between 2000-2013, according to the National Community Reinvestment Coalition (NCRC) report of 2019. A more recent report puts DC 13th on the national list: "Gentrification continued there, but it surged elsewhere."

All told, DC lost 80,000 Black residents between the years 2000 and 2020, according to the U.S. Census. Black residents dropped from 60% of DC's population in 2000 to 41.4% in 2020, while white residents rose from 30% of the population in 2000 to 39.6% in 2020.

38

Driving Forces

"DC 101: Housing and Development" offered a brief overview of residential real estate development:

> ...the reason DC is developing so quickly is that, in addition to local investors, we've got international investors from all over the world... some well-known universities invest their endowments through money-bundlers that fund gentrification in DC.... Money is made is by displacing and breaking down apartments, tearing down something that exists. (New units to be discussed, separately, below.)

> What is incentivized when the decision-making is about making the most money is directly at odds with what is affordable for people. Especially for families -- families with several children get hurt the most in this scheme. (See graphic below)
> -- Beth Wagner, Serve Your City DC

One current example cited is Brookland Manor in Northeast DC. It is the largest affordable housing community left in DC -- with 3-, 4-, and 5-bedroom unit -- but DC government has already approved and funded the owners' plan to create 1300 luxury apartments, tripling density and eliminating larger units. Residents and other community members say this plan threatens their close-knit community, built over decades, and have been resisting. Learn more from Brookland Manor Coalition.

Ward 5 Councilmember Kenyan McDuffie arranged for study of the housing stock and learned that the rarest resource in DC today is multi-bedroom, "family-sized" units. (Report available from DC's Deputy Mayor for Planning and Economic Development)

Text version of graphic:

1) Take an apartment occupied by low to moderate income families. $ (One) = monthly rent. One 3-room graphic with 2 adults, 2 children.

2) Displace them through rent hikes, redevelopment, or eviction. No $ = empty apartment. Family standing outside 3-room graphic.

3) Split the apartment into smaller units; rent to wealthy young professionals. $$$$$$ = monthly rent $$ + monthly rent $$ + monthly rent $$

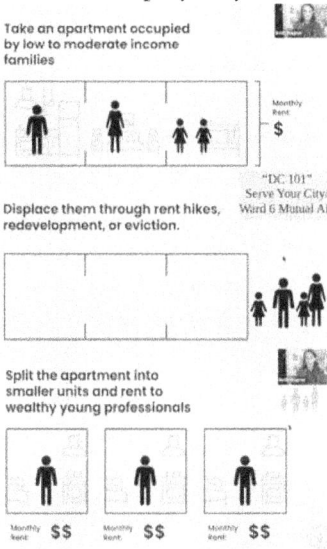

Take an apartment occupied by low to moderate income families

Displace them through rent hikes, redevelopment, or eviction.

Split the apartment into smaller units and rent to wealthy young professionals

Another Process

Another displacement process begins with building of new housing units, rather than breaking up existing homes:

1) Public land is given to private developers who...

2) build luxury housing, with minimal -- and sometimes less than promised -- affordable units; this creates...

3) extreme rent burdens, leading people to seek...

4) public housing or housing vouchers, but lack of resources and long waitlists bring people to the last resort:

5) ...homelessness.

-- Jillian Burford, Serve Your City DC

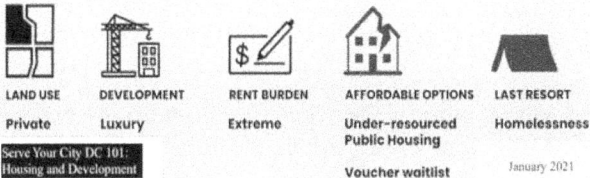

LAND USE	DEVELOPMENT	RENT BURDEN	AFFORDABLE OPTIONS	LAST RESORT
Private	Luxury	Extreme	Under-resourced Public Housing	Homelessness
			Voucher waitlist	January 2021

Serve Your City DC 101: Housing and Development

Graphic description: [map graphic] LAND USE Private >
[crane graphic] DEVELOPMENT Luxury >
[checkbook] RENT BURDEN Extreme >
[house graphic] AFFORDABLE OPTIONS Under-resourced Public Housing;
Voucher waitlist > [text graphic] LAST RESORT Homelessness

Community members in Southwest are studying the contribution of specific developers to this process. A report from Southwest Voice DC (March
2021) looks at equity results of 16 years of PN Hoffman developments.
See also: SW DC Action.

Last Resort

The displacement processes described above contribute to homelessness as
a last resort. Many chronically homeless people are facing other challenges
as well. In addition, responses that look like "solutions," such as DC's
"rapid housing voucher" system, can turn out to be temporary fixes at best.

See, e.g., "An 11-year-old uprooted from a gentrifying city" in the Post
(1/14/20), regarding what happens when the year of "rapid housing" support dries up, and this piece which focuses on who is (still) without housing, "Homelessness in DC fell..." on DCist (4/29/21):

> There was only a slight reduction in single individuals experiencing
> homelessness counted—3,947 single individuals were counted in
> 2020, compared to 3,871 individuals in 2021—which The Com-
> munity Partnership says is likely attributable to D.C.'s eviction ban.

> The count also showed significant disparities in who is experiencing
> homelessness in the District. 86.5% of all adults experiencing
> homelessness were Black, although just under half of all residents
> in D.C. are Black. 4.9% of people identified as Hispanic or Latinx.
> -- Chelsea Cirruzzo, DCist "Homelessness in DC Fell..."

For a discussion that includes pan-
demic-related specifics, including
eviction moratoria, see transcript or
listen to reporter Martin Auster-
muhle on "The Takeaway" in May
2021.

Tent encampments have grown in
DC in recent years. Image (row of
tents along an underpass) is a long-
standing encampment in area of DC, now called "NoMa" (for "north of
Mass. Ave") in September 2020. Throughout the pandemic, Serve Your City
DC/Ward 6 Mutual Aid (source of image) and a collection of advocacy

and aid groups devoted resources in support of people in NoMA and other encampments.

Some residents of luxury dwellings and other properties near encampments have clashed with advocates and with people living in tents over issues of hygiene, safety, and the right to use public land. In addition, those promot-

ing DC's retail growth see people living in tents as contrary to the image the City seeks to project.
(Image: Douglas Development, 1500 N Capitol; white couple appear through large coffeeshop window; a bicycle and cyclist in sunglasses behind shop lighting.)

When crime and violence occur in the vicinity of those who are experiencing housing instability, popular and official response is frequently to declare that "the problem" is the presence of a shelter, a tent encampment, or residents using housing vouchers. This attempt to criminalize poverty has dangerous consequences for many.

City officials have tried to provide some housing options while clearing encampments. There is debate, among all concerned, about specific numbers. Observers seem to agree that some people have been displaced without better prospects. The "clearing" process also results in loss of possessions, for people who have very few, and endangers physical and mental safety.

Despite the CDC's public health guidance against removing encampments and efforts of advocates and some DC Councilmembers, the city's response is still to "beautify" public land and to promote "no tent zones." The result is often fenced-off, unused areas or, as in the photo here, an underpass once sheltering people now blocked by cement barriers.

A Different Vision

At the start of the pandemic, advocates from and for DC's unhoused community noted that the number of vacant luxury apartments in the city, estimating that it roughly equaled the number of unhoused people at the time. Especially prior to vaccines, the key tools available to stop the spread of the virus were:

- physical distancing,
- ability to quarantine safely if necessary, and
- access to good facilities for hygiene.

Vacancy to Virus Reduction (V2VR) proposed using empty units for un-housed people, as a simple -- if radical-sounding -- virus reduction approach. While vaccination and shifts in the pandemic has changed the picture to some degree, the basic arguments still apply to promoting virus reduction and housing for all, for the long haul.

V2VR has yet to gain much traction, although the campaign was discussed on We Act Radio's "Community thru Covid" program and promoted through Serve Your City DC and other programs.

V2VR (v2vr.info) was presented to "DC 101: Housing and Development" by Reginald Black, Advocacy Director of People for Fairness Coalition, voting member of DC's Interagency Council on Homelessness, artist and contributor to Street Sense Media, and member of People Power Action.

In addition to providing a creative solution to an urgent problem, V2VR is an example of attempting to re-envision distribution of resources in new ways and of taking direction from those with relevant lived experience.

from Vacant to Virus Reduction image: Black man in glasses and baseball cap appears in Zoom box, labeled "Reginald Black," in top right corner of slide.

Main slide is stylized apartment grid showing stick-figure icons in sleep, eating, exercise, and other poses. Text reads: Covid-19 spreads rapidly. People in communal homeless shelters and congregate detention facilities are at grave risk. DC should house these people in the District's 10,000 vacant units.

1. Everyone must social distance to stop the spread of COVID19.
2. Housing is a human right and need.
3. Housing is physical healthcare.
4. Housing is mental and emotional healthcare.
5. Homelessness and incarceration are expensive.

Rereading Exodus

Economic "Not Knowing"

In Genesis, all of *Mitzrayim* express gratitude for the agricultural arrangements Joseph engineers. People who had been worried about starvation appear secure and well-provisioned in the new, centrally-planned economy. How do things go so wrong at the beginning of Exodus?

Suppose, for thought-experiment, that the gratitude expressed in Gen 47 is genuine and that the economy is operating to support everyone in *Mitzrayim*, including strangers, even during a famine, for an extended period. Then...

...(1) over time, a new cadre of administrators develops. Power corrupts, as power does, and the needs of society's most vulnerable, nearer to the margins, once protected by Joseph, are subordinated to those closer to Pharaoh in status -- until a whole segment of the population is, itself, viewed as expendable.

...(2) over time, a new cadre of administrators develops. Conflict arises, as conflict does, and Joseph's affinity for those at the margins, particularly those known as Hebrews or *Yisrael-ites*, is replaced with calls to unite -- until a whole segment of the population is, itself, viewed as a fly in the ointment.

...(3) over time, a new cadre of administrators develops. Racism surfaces, as racism does, and Joseph's assimilation is now viewed as suspect while tolerance is supplanted by desire for hegemony -- until the Hebrews/*Yisrael-ites* are now seen as threatening by their very existence.

Perhaps Pharaoh's "not knowing Joseph" means one or more of these processes at work, with the result that a whole segment of society -- once invited to dwell and tend after the crown's cattle -- is now viewed as expendable, an obstacle to profitable plans, and a threat.

Historical Patterns

Jews have faced a similar pattern in places like Spain and Poland throughout history. Jews in Europe were accused of spreading leprosy or plague and other crimes, resulting in mass eviction and murder of Jews plus "welcome elimination of any debt owed to Jewish moneylenders" (see bibliography).

In his "The ABCs of Slavery," the Joseph chapter in his bible tales, Dick Gregory explores Joseph's incarceration and interpretation of dreams for fellow inmates (Gen 40), suggesting "maybe Joseph was a Black cat":

> The butler in the Joseph story symbolizes America's treatment of Black folks. The butler used Joseph's talent as an interpreter of dreams and he promised to tell Pharaoh about Joseph. As soon as

the butler got himself comfortably back in Pharaoh's palace, he forgot about his word to Joseph.

America was built on the sweat, toil, and talent of Black folks. But when the work was done and the talent utilized, America quickly forgot its debt to Blacks. Black folks helped lay down the railroad tracks, but they could only work as porters after the trains started running. Black slaves picked the cotton, but the garment industry belonged to white folks. -- *Dick Gregory's Bible Tales*, p.73

DC Historical Displacement

Economics, ethics, and consequences of sweeping resettlement -- in biblical context and in history, from ancient examples to U.S. "Urban Renewal" -- is an enormous topic. Without trying to draw exact parallels from bible to DC history, consider a few examples of resettlement raised in "DC 101."

Nacotchtank people lost three-quarters of their population in just four decades. Beginning in 1608, with the first known European contact, the majority of the Nacotchank people, and others who had been living on land we now call "Washington, DC," were displaced or felled by disease and war. Some remaining Nacotchtank joined neighboring tribes, including the Piscataway Conoy.

Two major resettlements are outlined in a 2016 Urban Institute report:

> 1940s: Barry Farms, a community developed at the end of the Civil War by 500 freed Black families, is largely demolished to create space for public housing and is further devastated by the decision to have Suitland Parkway cut through the community, destroying individual and community assets.

> 1960s–70s: Urban renewal sweeps cities "clean." DC's largely Black southwest neighborhoods are targeted by eminent domain. More than 500 acres are bulldozed, along with 1,500 businesses—including many Black-owned businesses—and 6,000 homes. Approximately 23,000 residents, predominantly Black, are displaced with little compensation. The 5,800 new homes are to be inhabited by 13,000 middle- and upper-middle-class residents.
> -- *The Color of Wealth in the Nation's Capital*, 2016

DC also saw additional resettlement and destruction events, plus less formal displacement. Results include, according to that Urban Institute report: White DC households with net worth **81 (eighty-one) times** that of Black households. Building here, movement there, on it's own may not look like oppression.... but the overall result is clear.

Images of Martin Luther King Jr. Ave, SE

"Historic Anacostia Storefronts"

Images: Google Street Views of 2012 and 2017.

2012 Right to Left:
1918 MLK, light-colored aged storefront,
We Act Radio decal on window and "Cole's Cafe" sign over door;
1916 empty with Douglas Development's for-lease banner above door;
empty corner lot, with chain-link fence.

2017 Right to Left:
1922 MLK, District Culture;
1920 MLK, Check-IT; 1
1918 We Act Radio, with new black facade and old sign gone, "We Act Radio" in free-standing letters on overhang.
(1916 and adjacent empty lot, to the left, not visible in image).

Economics of Genesis and Exodus

The economics of Genesis and early Exodus play out in commercial real estate, too: One day invited to tend the ruler's cattle; the next, told to clear off.

In DC and around the country, property owners in under-valued areas gladly house funkier enterprises for lower rent. Gleeful celebration of local culture and business is regularly part of the deal.... until markets shift. Then "not knowing Joseph" manifests, with local concerns eclipsed in the face of higher sale prices or more upscale tenants. This pattern is often treated as an inevitable aspect of capitalism, thus normalizing the perspective that some segments of the economy can be viewed as expendable, obstacles to profit.

Businesses owned by two Cross River Dialogue participants were nearly lost to this cycle. The story is offered here as an illustration of the precarious line between stability and displacement -- even if this one does have something of a happy ending, so far.

Historic Anacostia Storefronts:

1) In 2011, We Act Radio moved into the former Cole's Cafe, 1918 MLK Avenue, SE. The previous occupant's name was still visible above the station's window, when Douglas Development obtained the next door property in 2012. (see images on previous page)

2) 1916 MLK had a series of short-term tenants -- temporary tax-prep, campaign office (Bowser for mayor '14), barbershop, etc. -- with empty periods between. 6Co Eatery moved in during 2021.)

3) Check-IT moved into 1920 MLK in 2015.

4) District Culture operated at 1922 MLK, until its owner was killed (2018).

5) Then, in 2019, the owner of the three buildings, 1918-1922 MLK, saw profit possibilities and sought to sell, which would displace existing tenants and thereby obliterate years of individual and collective investment in Historic Anacostia.

CRD participants and others mobilized for an alternative arrangement. Several Dialoguers testified to the DC Council's Business and Economic Development Committee. The committee seemed to agree that losing the three storefronts to another chain store -- which many feared would lead to domino-development all the way down MLK Avenue -- should be avoided. The committee, then full Council approved a grant for purchase of 1918-1922 MLK, making possible the new Go-Go Museum and next door DC

Pocket, while preserving We Act Radio... along with the jointly managed garden space behind the three storefronts.

Collective Community Space. When We Act Radio moved into 1918 MLK, the back lot was a mix of gravel, weeds, broken glass and needles. The space was only accessible through rear doors of 1918, 1920, or 1922, or by climbing a retaining wall. It was invisible from the street, so a haven for illegal activity.

We Act Radio gathered volunteers to clean it up and begin a garden. Later Check-IT Enterprises and District Culture joined the effort. Years of collective work transformed an eyesore and health hazard into a meeting and performance space, full of

Wooden fencing and raised garden beds in otherwise empty lot behind 1918 MLK Avenue (2013).

Over the years, the "Secret Garden," in various states of development -- from gravel to garden to deck and stage -- hosted meetings, concerts, parties, and, all too often, memorial gatherings...including the one (pictured here) for Christopher Barry, August 2016.

Memorial gathering for Marion "Christopher" Barry in Secret Garden.

Image description follows section.

The weekend of 5/25-28/18 at the Secret Garden included a Friday party with an announcement of further plans for the space.... Hours later, District Culture owner, Alexander "Bundy" Mosby (z'') was shot to death outside his home. A few days later, hundreds gathered in the same space for a public forum to address gun violence. Still later, a mural was added, naming the garden for Bundy.

Many of these activities were advertised and/or reported in local media. The garden space was discussed in public testimony to the DC Council. But Douglas Development apparently took no notice, not checking on the space when it was neglected or during its transformations over the years....Until early 2021.

With construction on nearby buildings underway, an access query brought Douglas Development's attention to that odd space and their ownership of it. Douglas Jemal said at one point in the ensuing controversy that his company "had forgotten" the property. Once reminded, the developer opted to exercise his rights. His lawyers sent Ronald Moten, who by then owned 1918-20-22 MLK, a "cease and desist" order regarding the space. The planting beds, deck, stage, and other improvements of the Bundy Secret Garden would have to go. (Image: Community Event 2021; description follows section.)

Check-IT, We Act Radio, Serve Your City DC, and others organized in protest and petition....

....What Jemal or anyone else would do with the lot -- which still has no access by street or alley or, with new construction, via retaining wall -- was never clarified. Still, the developer could have pressed his claim to the space. Instead....

Jemal and Moten held a joint press event at which Jemal said he was grateful for community work on the space and glad to "give something back," adding "The Secret Garden is not a secret anymore." Community use of the collective space, so far, continues.

Through concerted effort and a variety of connections -- in political and financial arenas -- three storefronts in Downtown Historic Anacostia escaped sale and likely demolition. Three businesses, owned or co-owned by local Black entrepreneurs, continued to operate. And the community space survived. Meanwhile, however, the immediate vicinity is changing drastically, as long-planned development in the area takes shape. And development visions do not appear to include We Act Radio, Check-IT/Go-Go Museum, or DC Pocket -- or existing community members.

Moten often asks: "Will all this development benefit the people who were here when nobody else wanted to be?"

40

Part of the Vision?

The developer for "MLK Gateway," at the corner of Good Hope Road (to the left in the rendering) and MLK Avenue (straight ahead), has for years been presenting a vision for the area with no trace of current tenants. The Menkiti Group emphasizes hiring contractors who are local and Black-owned and prioritizing local people for construction. Moreover, one new tenant is Enlightened, Inc., a minority-owned technology business. But the vision does not include existing neighbors on MLK or Good Hope Road.

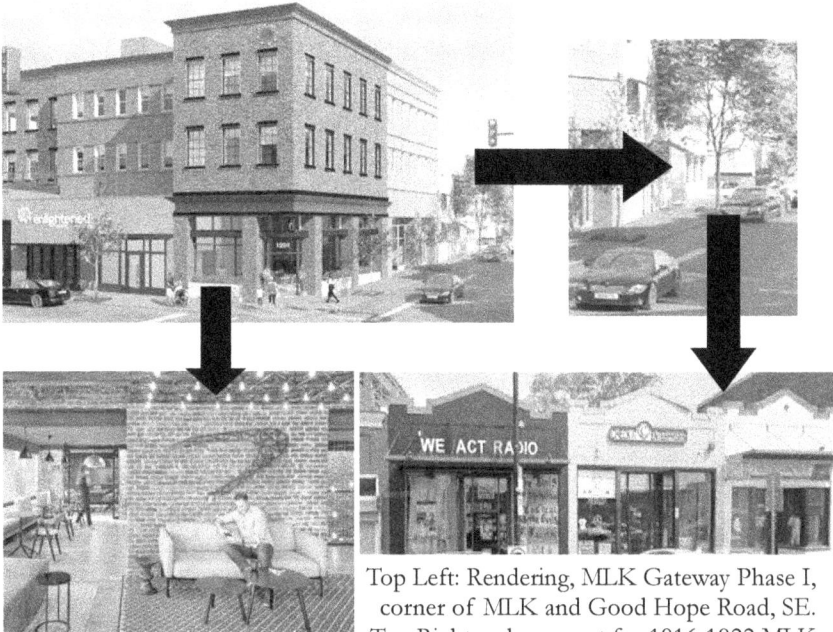

Top Left: Rendering, MLK Gateway Phase I, corner of MLK and Good Hope Road, SE.
Top Right: enlargement for 1916-1922 MLK
Below Right: current street view of 1918-1920-1922
Below Left: Developer's ad for Capital One Cafe in the new Gateway building
Descriptions follow section .

Those shiny white, nameless buildings, in the middle of the block on MLK, are situated in place of We Act Radio and neighbors. Renderings are often devoid of detail, of course, so perhaps this one did not intentionally erase existing operations. But the developer advertises for tenants with a map that omits most going concerns, including We Act Radio and Check-IT, while presenting Capital One Cafe as a place with customers who look nothing like most of the people doing businesses on Good Hope and MLK over the last decade or more. This is the vision Menkiti chose to present, and it's what the City is promoting.

If this is the vision the City is promoting, why wouldn't owners of nearby real estate -- 1918-20-22 MLK Avenue or any other property -- follow suit and treat existing people and operations as expendable?

IMAGE DESCRIPTIONS

Memorial, Aug 2016: Amid leafy produce and dirt, a small gathering of Black people, some in folding chairs, some perched on low fence, face a speaker behind a microphone stand and memorial photo. In background is rear of a commercial building (without identifying marks but recognizable as 1918 MLK to those who've been there).

Community Event, Jan 2021: Center of photo is full band in winter coats on wooden stage (Tru Worshiperz Band&Ministry, Gospel Go-Go). Stage reads "Cole's [Cafe -- the sign once atop 1918 MLK]. Background mural reads "Preserve Statehood" and shows Rep Eleanor Holmes Norton on one side and another head [Petey Greene] with large 1970s sunglasses, barely visible behind band. Foreground shows wooden deck and with small metal fire pit.

MLK Gateway materials:

Rendering of three-story commercial building on corner, with glass-heavy retail space on ground-floor and offices above. To the left is with another three-story set of buildings, with commercial space on the ground floor, one business labeled "Enlightened." Behind the Gateway building is a second new office structure with street retail followed, mid-block by a set of unidentifiable smaller buildings.

Enlargement: mid-block view, showing the blank white facades not reflecting current (or past 15 years) at 1916-1922 MLK.

Developer's ad for Capital One Cafe -- upscale setting with only white customers.

Inset: We Act Radio, Check-IT (Go-Go Museum), and DC Pocket today.

Pharaoh's Policy Decisions

Considering who is part of a land's past and who is envisioned in its future raises important questions around resistance and reparations -- topics for later stages. For now, look at some of Pharaoh's early policy decisions:

- First, he set up taskmasters and forced labor, "But the more they were oppressed, the more they increased...." (Ex 1:11-12);

- Then, ruthless labor and making life bitter, apparently without desired effect (Ex 1:13-14);

- Next, the midwives are told to kill baby boys; but they tell Pharaoh *Yisrael-ite* women give birth too quickly for them to attend (Ex 1:15-21);

- Finally, Pharaoh commands all the people: "Every boy that is born, you are to cast him (off) [*tashlikhuhu*] into The River," but that doesn't quite work as expected either (Ex 1:22ff).

At this point in the story, incredulity often arises: arises: "Can we imagine any people behaving as Pharaoh directs toward *Yisrael-ite* babies?"

Pharaoh's command (Exod 1:22) is often translated as tossing or throwing ("casting") baby boys into The River. But biblical scholar Adele Berlin notes that the verb here is the same one used when Hagar leaves Ishmael under the bush (Gen 21:15) and in other verses where the meaning is "to abandon" ("cast off"). She compares ancient Greek practice of leaving baby girls on hillsides to die out of sight of the parents, saying that here, on the water:

> The predictable -- but not immediate -- result would be the baby boy's death.
> -- commentary in *Torah: A Women's Commentary* (URJ, 2008)

Predictable, but not immediate....

"Can we imagine any people behaving as Pharaoh directs toward *Yisrael-ite* babies?" Isn't the history of DC land use a set of decisions with predictable, if not immediate, results leading to extreme harm for many?

Urban Renewal, mentioned briefly above had an enormous impact on DC's housing landscape, particularly in Southwest, where neighborhoods were destroyed in creation of the Southwest Freeway and government offices, and in Southeast, where displaced people were relocated, leading to further displacement. Displacing grown people from one neighborhood to another is not identical to tossing babies in the river, but it has predictable, if not immediate, results leading to health, education, and safety outcomes that shorten life. Life expectancy in whiter and wealthier parts of DC is 23 years longer than that in predominantly Black neighborhoods. Decades of life.

Moreover, DC's policy and spending decisions today continue to make the city more comfortable for some, especially those with the most resources, and far less welcoming to many, including the most vulnerable among us. As discussed above, DC's housing policies promote the reduction of affordable housing and the consequent displacement of lower income people. Resulting, for too many, in a lack of stable, safe shelter. The results of such policy and spending may not be immediate, but they are predictable and dangerous.

Predictable Results

The opening of the Exodus story frequently elicits a "How could people behave that way?!" reaction, as noted at the start of this section. The same reaction is common in response to many points in history, as though people in our own time, or society or particular social group, are incapable of bigotry and violence. Or maybe it's just ourselves, individually, who are somehow more enlightened? As considered in this stage of the journey, however, people can and do regularly take steps with predictable, if not immediate, results leading to extreme harm.

The displacement processes described in this stage are underway all around us. We must learn to recognize the various steps in the process and understand the predictable, if not immediate results.... And then find ways to ameliorate harmful results while simultaneously dismantling systems and processes that lead there.

This process has been unfolding in DC -- and probably wherever you live if it's not here -- for a long time. And one of the ways people do, indeed "behave that way," is by accepting steps that may seem arguably harmless considered alone.

Why shouldn't the owner of a property sell to the highest bidder? obtain the highest rent the market will bear? The City adopts Comprehensive Plans and Racial Equity guidelines, but the engines of profit continue to chug along, as both public and private building fuels displacement in DC.

Private Profits

For example, in Southwest, thousands of new, luxury units were built in the last twenty years with only a small percentage of affordable units, and even fewer deeply affordable and/or with multiple bedrooms. Douglas Development alone is responsible for over 1000 luxury units in Southwest in recent years, with only 61 of that total affordable at any level. Just eleven affordable apartments are included in the 453 units at 1900 Half Street, which is already completed.

Development on public DC land requires 30% affordable housing. DC's Inclusionary Zoning now requires, for new private residential construction, at least 8-10% housing affordable at 50-80% of Median Family Income (formerly: Area Median Income).

Cotton Annex was approved with 50 affordable units – the minimum allowable -- all at 50-80% of MFI.

DC's 2021 MFI was $129K. 50-80% MFI is $64-$103K. Median income for Black households in Ward 6 is $52K – and only three other wards have higher median incomes for Black households.

In process are another 610 units at the Cotton Annex, 300 12th Street, with the bare minimum of "affordable" units (see box). After obtaining zoning approval, Douglas opted to sell (at $45 million for property bought at $30.3 million); California-based Carmel Partners reduced the total number of units maintaining the affordable percentage.

The long-term result of such building has been a serious displacement of lower income Southwest residents, with a strong racial imbalance: loss of 1600 Black (-21%) and gain of 4600 white (+157%) residents in the last decade. More generally, the District is failing to meet its affordable housing goals across all income levels.

Image descriptions for "Selling the City"

page 117

Screen-shot from Douglas website for 1378 H NE
Image: two-story townhome renovated as a bar with balcony for seating, reads "Rose DeJavu" over door and on glass door, decorated with a red rose. To the left are more townhomes, apparently abandoned. To the east, an empty restaurant space still bearing a large sign, "Ohio Restaurant: Southern Style Home Cooking," topped by satellite dishes.

Douglas 501 H NE flyer
Image descriptions: Four-photo mosaic, clockwise from top left: 1) behind a wrought- iron fence, four young white people sit together outdoors, relaxing; summer clothing, one t-shirt reads on back "Rendon 6." 2) three levels of retail, shiny white structure with large tinted windows; upper residential stories (28 units) of amber-colored structure with windows and balconies. 3) Capitol Bikeshare station. 4) just a corner visible of closer view of two stories of the retail structure -- mostly windows visible, no people.

page 118

Douglas 1500 N Capitol flyer
Image description: On the left, neighborhood map superimposed with the words "THE LOCATION: 1500." Below in small print, probably not legible to most are population and income statistics. On the right is view through large plate glass into a coffee shop where a cyclist with brown skin is seated alone, not far from a couple with white skin, a man looking at a woman, and the woman smiling at the camera through the glass.

Pharaoh-Moses-Midwives Unite

Several years ago, Marc Dollinger, author of *Black Power, Jewish Politics*, told NPR's Leah Donella:

> One of my African-American colleagues, he said, "If I ever go to a Seder and the Jews say that they know what it's like because they too were once slaves in Egypt," he's gonna punch 'em.

> Because if Jews have to go back to ancient Egypt to get the slavery metaphor, then they've kind of missed that American Jewish history is a story of rapid social ascent, and African-American history is the legacy of slavery....
> -- "Exploding Myths about 'Black Power, Jewish Politics'" (6/4/18)

This does not mean that we cannot learn from the Exodus story or from the Passover experience and subsequent journey through the wilderness. It does mean, however, that we need to exercise caution in how we do so.

Earlier in this journey, *Rereading Exodus* suggested asking how we are like various characters in the Exodus narrative. This is a good time to return to these questions and apply them in an outward fashion, to our life and work:

- Where are we trying to stand up to power, like the midwives?

- Where are we struggling with identity and relationship to power, like Moses?

- Where have we, like Pharaoh, forgotten Joseph?

- Where are we, like different groups in Genesis and Exodus, benefitting from someone else's long-ago land grab?

As we consider what look like Pharaoh's policies, ahead, we can ask how dynamics from the Exodus story are operating in the world around us. We can ask what (mix of) Exodus roles we are playing. And we can begin to explore how identifying oppressive structures might help us dismantle them.

Predictable Infant and Maternal Mortality

A previous section introduced a commentary on Pharaoh's edict about tossing babies into The River (Exod 1:22). Biblical scholar Adele Berlin noted parallels with the ancient Greek practice of leaving infant girls on a hillside, to die out of sight of their parents:

> The predictable -- but not immediate -- result would be the baby boy's death.
> -- Berlin, in *Torah: A Women's Commentary* (URJ, 2008)

The Land Use chapter explored ways in which District policy, historically and current, allows "predictable -- but not immediate -- result[s]" that lead to displacement and death. In this stage, we consider predictable results that are even more immediate and at least as stark.

A recent (2012-16) study by the DC Department of Health, the infant mortality rate (per 1000 live births) in DC was as follows

- for non-Hispanic white mothers: 2.55

- for Hispanic mothers: 5.33

- for non-Hispanic black mothers: 11.49

- see map by ward

The map, from the DOH study cited above, shows a distinct pattern of higher-to-lower infant mortality from east-to-west in DC. Babies are lost in Wards 5, 7, and 8 -- with higher Black and lower income populations -- at three and four times the rate lost in in wealthier and whiter areas. Specifics:

Ward 8: 9.33 or greater
Wards 7 and 5: 5.8-9.32
Wards 6 and 1: 5.15-5.79
Ward 4: 2.28-5.14
Wards 2 and 3: 2.27 or less

The pattern persisted in 2019 statistics (most recent available).

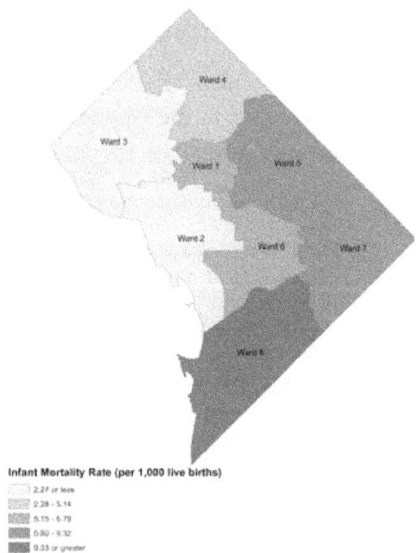

Figure 26. Infant Mortality Rate by Ward, District of Columbia 2012-2016

Infant Mortality Rate (per 1,000 live births)
- 2.27 or less
- 2.28 - 5.14
- 5.15 - 5.79
- 5.80 - 9.32
- 9.33 or greater

The maternal death rate for black women in the U.S. is more than double that for white women, according to U.S. Centers for Disease Control. The maternal death rate in DC is roughly twice the national average, with large and persistent disparities across race.

This graphic from the Centers for Disease Control compares states with lowest PRMR (pregnancy-related mortality ratios), medium, and highest PRMR. Disparities displayed are 3.0, 3.3, and 2.8 when comparing white and black women in these groups of states.

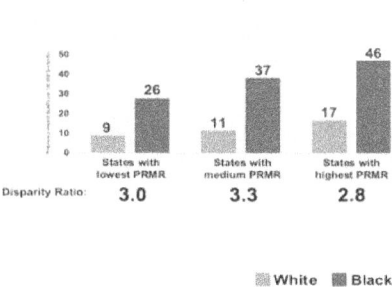

In addition, according to the National Committee for Responsive Philanthropy, Black women are more likely to

- Be uninsured before becoming pregnant.
- Be exposed to environmental risks.
- Receive subpar medical care based on their location.
- Experience racial bias from health care providers.

None of this is new. The results have long been predictable.

Predictable Planning

There is currently no facility to assist in delivery of babies east of the Anacostia River in the nation's capitol. To be extra clear and make no mistake:

- In the United States capitol city, 20% of the population lives where there is no facility to assist in delivery of babies.

- In a country and city where it has long been known that Black mothers and babies suffer mortality at much higher rates than their white counterparts, Black mothers and babies are left without essential care.

- In a city where 20% of the population makes more than $200,000/ year and another 18% earn between $125,000 and $200,000, the government has managed to leave a substantial portion of the population without access to key medical care, including obstetrics.

- **There has been no facility to assist in delivery of babies east of the Anacostia River in the nation's capitol for four years. There won't be one for another three years, although ground just broke on the new hospital.**

DC's Department of Health mapped distribution of hospital and surgical services in 2017:

Nine hospitals west of the river and two east [one of the two is a psychiatric facility].

Five ambulatory surgical centers west of the river. DOH Map annotated here with "I" for Level I Trauma Center -- all four west of the river.

Three important updates since 2017:

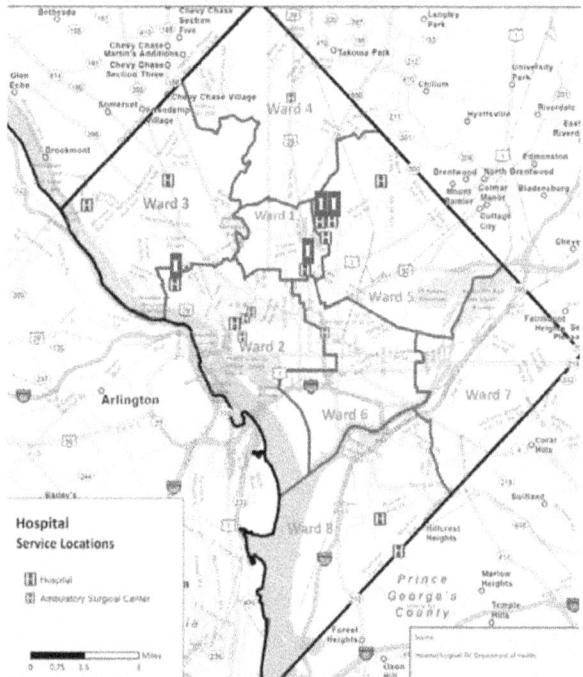

1) United Medical Center, on the southeast border, closed its obstetrics department in 2017. UMC is slated to close entirely in 2023.

2) Providence, that lone hospital in the Northeast quadrant, west of the river, closed in May 2019.

3) The City plans to build a new hospital in Ward 8, which is scheduled to open in 2025. It is slated to include a Level III Trauma Center, despite decades of advocacy for a Level I Trauma Center east of the river.

Entering a Level I or Level II Trauma Center increases a gunshot victim's survival chance by 25% -30%. And survival decreases with distance from such a facility. Victims of traffic accidents also fare substantially better with quick access to a Level I or II Trauma Center. Yet DC has refused community demands for equity in distribution of these centers, leaving all four west of the river.

To be extra clear and make no mistake:

- In the United States capitol city, 20% of the population lives where the best they can expect -- even as a new hospital is planned -- is a Level III trauma center.

- In a city where gun violence has long been more prevalent east of the river, the City is planning -- actively, purposefully -- to leave the area most affected by gun violence without a shooting victim's best chance of survival.

- In a city where a greater proportion of traffic accidents take place east of the river, the District has chosen -- actively, purposefully -- to leave the area most affected by life-threatening car crashes without a victim's best chance of survival.

- **In a City where access to health supports of all kinds have long been egregiously uneven, the plan is to leave those most in need with less -- again. Still.**

Trauma Centers and DC

The American College of Surgeons verifies trauma centers after they have "successfully completed a verification visit." Trauma centers are designated at levels I-V, where I has the highest level of resources.

DC now calls the planned east of the river hospital a "verified trauma center," with on level specified. Using "verified," years before the hospital is even open (and so ready for verification visit) is premature; omitting "Level III," when that is what is planned, is obfuscation....
...and an insult, suggesting as it does that stakeholders either do not care what level of resources are to be provided or will be fooled into thinking "verified" somehow means more than it does.

The City's approach has been "shrouded in mystery, and there is no transparency," say Ambrose Lane, Jr. (Ward 7 Health Alliance etal, see above). He argues that the administration must be more specific in conversations with the community. In addition, the Ward 7 Health Alliance has been advocating for a small Level I or Level II Trauma Center in Ward 7 as well as a larger Level I facility in Ward 8 – where current plans call for only Level III in Ward 8 and nothing in Ward 7.

Amanda Michelle Gomez City Desk reporter, Washington City Paper has covered this story over the years. See also WAMU's Kojo Nnamdi show, 9/20/19, for example.

Pharaoh's Household

The plague of blood symbolizes a tragic reality....

Pharaoh was willing to negotiate in earnest only after his own son was killed. Countless Hebrew mothers and fathers had lost sons. But Pharaoh only listened when death came to his own household. The loss of a loved one caused Pharaoh to change his oppressive ways.
-- *Dick Gregory's Bible Tales*, p.87 (full citation, author bio in Phase 2.5)

Gregory goes on to wonder "how many wars would be avoided if the loved ones of the national leaders were the first soldiers to face enemy fire?" But his commentary on Exodus applies just as clearly to loss of a loved one through drug overdose, illness, gun violence, or many avoidable causes.

What will it take for Pharaoh "to change his oppressive ways," in the context of health, beginning with DC.

44

Opioids

Yet Black people comprised over 80% of deaths due to opioids in DC, in recent years, although the population of the city is now only 46% Black. A few data specifics can be found on the next page. These can be summarized, however, by saying that deaths to opioids for Black people far outstrip those of white or Hispanic people -- at rates so that Black people are dying from opioids between four and ten times more often than white people in DC. Ward 3, our whitest and wealthiest ward, experienced less than ten deaths in any year between 2016 and 2021, according to the Medical Examiner. Wards 7 and 8, our predominantly Black wards east of the river, each suffered rates between six and ten times higher than Ward 3.

The District has long known that opioid overdose was concentrated in Wards 7 and 8 and has failed to provide needed resources, according to Ambrose Lane, Jr., founder of the Ward 7 Health Alliance. He adds that -- even after years of advocacy -- the City still lacks a plan for enhanced inclusion of east of the river pharmacies in the Live Long DC Program, and 24-hour healthcare providers for when overdoses occur. The only 24-hour treatment center is in deep Northwest.

In addition to his work with the Ward 7 Health Alliance, Lane is a 2022 candidate for DC Council At-Large and a Cross River Dialoguer.

Opioid death in DC by Race and Ward

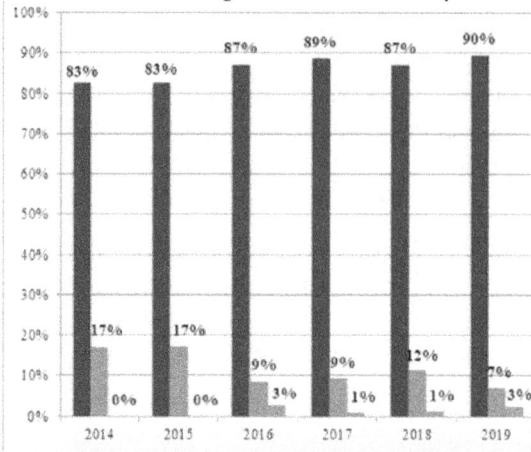

Graph at left shows DC statistics for 2014-2019. Black people made up 83 - 90% of deaths due to opioids while white and Hispanic people comprised far smaller percentages: 0-3% reported as Hispanic, and the following percentages white: 17, 17, 9, 9, 12, and 7%.

Data from DC's medical examiner show data by ward (below), with Ward 3 showing the lowest number of deaths, <10 in any year; followed by Ward 2, Ward 4, and Ward 1, in order, ranging from a high of 10-20 (with a 2020 spike in Ward 1, up to 26); then Ward 6 with between 19 and 38 deaths and Ward 5 with 28-44; Ward 7 and Ward 8 experienced, respectively, 33-53 and 32-74 deaths. .

Fig. 9: Number of Drug Overdoses due to Opioid Use by Ward of Residence and Year

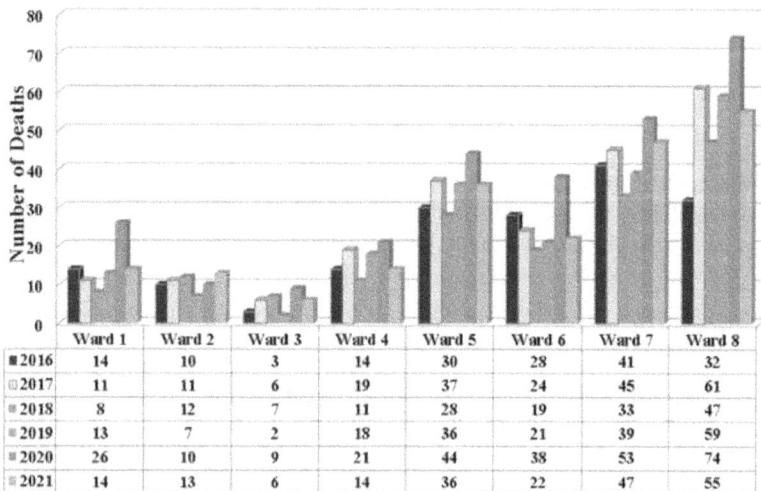

	Ward 1	Ward 2	Ward 3	Ward 4	Ward 5	Ward 6	Ward 7	Ward 8
2016	14	10	3	14	30	28	41	32
2017	11	11	6	19	37	24	45	61
2018	8	12	7	11	28	19	33	47
2019	13	7	2	18	36	21	39	59
2020	26	10	9	21	44	38	53	74
2021	14	13	6	14	36	22	47	55

Coronavirus

As previously noted, Black people are now 46% of DC's population. Yet, Black people have comprised 77% of deaths due to Covid-19, consistently throughout the pandemic. In addition, Black people have contracted Covid-19 at a rate more than twice that of white residents:

> 68,352 cases among Black people and
> 28,856 among white people.
> -- cumulative statistics for DC, from late January 2022

Data by ward follow the same pattern seen in hospitals, maternal and infant death, and other statistics shared so far: Wards 7 and 8, east of the river, and Ward 5, just west of the river in Northeast -- the three wards with the highest Black populations -- are hardest hit.

Racial disparities in Covid-19 cases and deaths were widely predicted, early in the pandemic from/for DC and the entire country. Those familiar with DC also predicted the specific disparity centered along the Anacostia River or between Ward 5, 7, and 8, on the one hand, and the rest of the city on the other.

Not every jurisdiction is transparent concerning race and coronavirus data, according to the very detailed information provided by Johns Hopkins University. DC had the data, confirming predictions, and continued with policy and practice that did not favor those most in need.

DC's system for obtaining a vaccine appointment, to take one crucial example, relied on access to a computer and reliable internet as well as freedom to focus on a time-consuming, and highly stressful, process. The graphic above shows vaccination rates (early 2021) in DC's wealthiest and whitest Ward 3 far exceeding those in Wards 7 and 8, while Ward 3 had one of the lowest death rates, Wards 7 and 8 among the highest. The graphic uses information from DC's Dept of Health and appeared in a March 2021 Washington Post story.

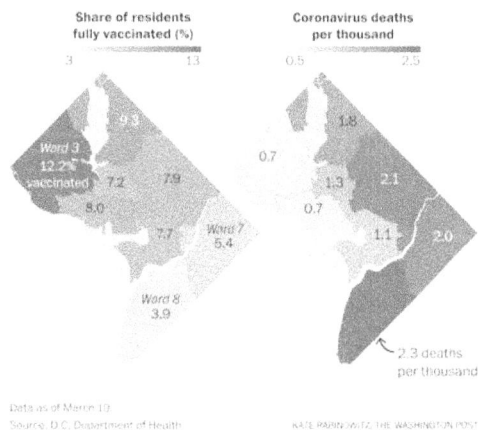

The District's Wards 7 and 8 have received the fewest vaccines, despite high coronavirus death rates

Share of residents fully vaccinated (%)

Coronavirus deaths per thousand

Data as of March 10
Source: D.C. Department of Health

KATE RABINOWITZ, THE WASHINGTON POST

Image description for this double-map follows.

Double-map image description: Two maps of DC divided into (2021) wards. Left-hand maps shows vaccination rates (early in 2021). Highest rate, 12.2%, in Ward 3, followed by Ward 4= 9.3%, Ward 5= 7.9%, Ward 6=7.7%, Ward 2 = 8.0%, Ward 1= 7.2%, while Ward 7=5.4% and Ward 8=3.9%. In a mapping system using lighter for less vaccinated, Wards 7 and 8, east of the river, stand out as far lighter than other wards.

Right-hand map shows deaths per thousand (early in 2021). Highest death rate, 2.3%, in Ward 8, followed closely by Ward 5=2.1 and Ward 7=2.0; Ward 6=1.1, Ward 4=1.8, Ward 2=1.3, Ward 1=0.7 and Ward 3=0.7. In a mapping system using darker for higher deaths, Wards 7 and 8, east of the river, and Ward 5, DC's other predominantly Black ward, stand out as far darker than western parts of the city.

"Pharaoh's Household" Data

Total Covid-19 Deaths by Race

	deaths	% of deaths	% of population
All	1289	Deaths as of late January 2022	
Black	1002	77%	46.0%
Hispanic/Latinx	116	8%	11.3%
Non-Hispanic White	114	8%	37.5%
Asian	16	1%	4.5%
Unknown	21	1%	
Other	10	1%	

Covid-19 Numbers in DC's Hardest Hit Wards

	Cases in hardest hit wards	Deaths in hardest hit wards
Ward 8	20,596	258
Ward 7	18,735	208
Ward 5	18,829	236

DC consistently reports such statistics sans denominator: Numbers of cases and deaths, e.g., without related population, or percentage of city residents, or other context. In addition, for clarity: As is common for DC coronavirus reporting, data sheets are not all updated at the same point. So five of the deaths counted in the previous table (1289 total) have not been added to this sheet.

DC's new Council Office of Racial Equity issued a detailed report on this topic in March 2021. When community organizers tried to address the growing racial gap in vaccination rates, however, their effort was nearly derailed: The plan was to promote vaccines offered by Howard University Hospital staff at a historically Black church, in an under-vaccinated neighborhood, with Black residents as the target audience; but some community members and local officials sought to "widen access," thereby nullifying any chance of closing the existing racial gap.

Those who supported the event as a Black-only vaccine clinic had to walk a fine legal line. In the end, one set of community volunteers organized to strongly request that anyone who was not in the primary target audience wait until the end of the event to receive a vaccine if any remained. Finally, many shots were distributed to Black residents who had previously been unable, or unwilling, to be vaccinated. But the event's envisioning, planning, and backlash illustrate the complexities of knowing there is a racial disparity, on the one hand, and obstacles that arise in acting to address it, even where there's a will.

Our systems continue to favor the privileged, the wealthy, and the white -- with deadly health results.

Gun Violence

In DC, as in many other areas, gun violence has long been concentrated in certain sections. The result is that some DC folks are in trauma and mourning nearly all the time, have been for decades, while people in other areas are -- or have the option of being -- unscathed. Since mid-2015, "Say This Name" website has been listing DC homicides to help individuals, groups, and especially congregations, mark the losses...and perhaps be led to address the causes.

The idea was similar to what Gregory expressed about Pharaoh's household -- that apathy would be impossible if local civic and communal leaders, from all over the city, took the losses as seriously is if the departed were someone close....

Table (below) of losses to homicide and guns in DC. Killings by police are included on the website, although they are usually not listed as "homicide" by the medical examiner. Overall numbers may strike people from cities like Chicago as small. For a town DC's size -- and particularly for those regularly less than six degrees of separation from shootings and death -- the numbers are huge.

And, of course, one violent death is too many.

Losses to Homicide or Killing by Police in Recent Years

Year	2021	2020	2019	2018
Losses to homicide or police	233	202	168	161
...of those, to guns (police or others)	193	178	136	123
incident in SE or NE	172	149	129	135
...of those, in Ward 7 or 8 specifically	140	114	**	**
departed resided in SE or NE	121	107	95	114

**Say This Name did not record ward data until 2020.

Oppressive Ways

Say This Name was launched so that the deaths in DC could be marked and mourned. Anecdotal evidence suggests that this is having some impact on how close, or distant, various communities feel toward the losses; whether and how this is influencing policy is not clear.

Meanwhile, on occasion, including during January 2022 when this book was being (re-)written, shootings take place in areas of DC less accustomed to carnage. Officials and many others with little to say about the city's regular losses to guns suddenly call for outrage and attention to the needs of those affected by gun violence.

From a direct health perspective, much information is missing in a list of deaths by gun:

- physical trauma of non-fatal shootings;
- resulting disability, temporary or chronic;
- psychological trauma for those involved, or witnessing, an incident;
- stress of regular proximity for to gun violence; and
- impact, especially on children, in ways we don't yet understand.

Some additional data is available, but for purposes here, we can extrapolate from the statistics above showing that Wards 7 and 8, along with Ward 5 -- DC's predominantly Black neighborhoods -- have been hardest hit in terms of all these areas.

Knowing is a big part of our collective job, as we re-read the Exodus story. It's not clear that data -- or data alone -- will get Pharaoh "to change his oppressive ways."

Stress

One way to understand the impact of that "millstone that is *Mitzrayim*" is to consider the impact of stress on health. DC 101, in their June 2021 presentation on Health, outlined a cycle that functions like that millstone: Persistent stress makes people sick.

>> Stressor (discrimination, social stress, financial stress) >>
Reaction to Stress >>
Wear & Tear on Body and Organ Systems >>
Reduced Optimum Health >>
Increased Sensitivity to Stress >>
(around again to) stressor >>

Graphic shows above stress-cycle in circular format.

From DC 101
Serve Your City/
W6 Mutual Aid

Many people, including Jews of all hues, experience discrimination of some kind, and many face social and/or financial stress. All that has an impact on health and is part of the "millstone that is *Mitzrayim*," until we get everyone out from under. However, Black people, in- and outside Jewish communities, are subjected to regular stresses that others do not directly experience.

Anti-Black racism -- both individual acts of racism and the effects of institutional racism on everyday life -- is one source of stress. In addition, institutional racism creates secondary sources:

- greater threat of negative or dangerous interaction with police;

- greater incidence of incarceration of a loved one;

- greater chance of facing, oneself or as a parent, school-based police interactions and other elements of the school-to-prison pipeline.

Add to these other factors which disproportionately affect Black people in DC:

- higher unemployment and less stable employment;

- poorer housing conditions, higher rent burdens and eviction threat;

- higher unemployment and less stable employment;

- greater distances from home to work and less reliable public transit;

- regular exposure to gun violence;

- more restricted availability of safe play and exercise areas;

- greater exposure to environmental hazards...

...the list goes on. The "millstone that is *Mitzrayim*" weighs heavily and constantly.

As noted earlier: Life expectancy overall in whiter and wealthier parts of DC is 23 years longer than that in predominantly Black neighborhoods. Comparing specific neighborhoods east of the river with far west of the river, the gaps are even larger. Decades of life.

And the gap is growing rather than closing.

Find all the "DC 101" programs on Serve Your City/Ward 6 Mutual Aid channels at Facebook and YouTube.

The Thunders Ceased

A series of worsening plagues are unleashed on *Mitzrayim* as Pharaoh re-
fuses to let the People go. The first plague turns The River to blood; the
tenth and final plague kills the firstborns, discussed above by Dick Gregory.
Several times before that final plague, Pharaoh seems to relent, telling
Moses and Aaron that the People can go but then changing his mind.

This pattern repeats:

46

→ plague

→ Pharaoh relents

→ plague stops

→ Pharaoh un-relents

→ new plague

Exploring this pattern can illuminate
some reasons it takes so long for
Pharaoh "to change his oppressive ways" and how data is involved.

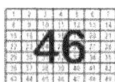

Sometimes the un-relenting
involves God hardening
Pharaoh's heart, and sometimes
Pharaoh hardens his own heart.
Two different verbs are used:
one related to "weight" [kavod,
כבד], and one related to
"strength" [chazak, חזק] There
is a huge body of discussion,
over centuries, about these
active and passive processes.

The seventh plague provides a helpful illustration. The plague of hail is
smiting man and beast, herbs and trees all over *Mitzrayim* -- except in Gos-
hen, where the *Yisrael-ites* live (Ex 9:23-26). In response, Pharaoh calls for
Moses and Aaron and says to them:

> 'I have sinned this time; YHVH is righteous, and I and my people
> are wicked. Entreat YHVH, and let there be enough of these
> mighty thunderings and hail; and I will let you go, and you shall stay
> no longer.' -- Ex 9:27-28

Pharaoh and all Mitzrayim had experienced the rain and the hail and "the
thunders [הקלות, ha-kolot]." The plague is understood by everyone in the
story, including Pharaoh, to be evidence of a state of affairs in need of correction. The evidence is convincing, and Pharaoh is resolved to act. Then --

> And when Pharaoh saw that the rain and the hail and the thunders
> [הקלות, ha-kolot] were ceased, he sinned yet more, and hardened his
> heart [וַיַּכְבֵּד לִבּוֹ, va-yachebed libo], he and his servants. -- Ex 9:34

When the evidence is no longer in front of him, Pharaoh's resolve falters.

Note, too, that the Hebrew word "*lev*" -- what Pharaoh or God hardens
in the biblical text -- is usually translated as "heart." But the biblical
meanings include "mind" and "will." Biblical language has no heart/mind
dichotomy, and the biblical "heart" is not related to modern notions of

romance. *Lev* is the source of thinking and decision-making. What Pharaoh hardens here could be determination, inclination, or resolution.

Disappearing Evidence

The previous section explored preventable health hazards, including illness, violence, and drug overdose, in which DC other locales see enormous gaps across race in terms of impact and outcome. This section touches on what happens when evidence regarding these hazards is unavailable.

As noted above, not all jurisdictions track Covid-19 data by race, which means that gaps in how different communities experience this pandemic might be overlooked. In addition, the U.S. is still recovering from decades of severely restricted funding for research on gun violence (see box); lack of data by race also affects how this epidemic is understood.

Gun Violence Research

For nearly 25 years, U.S. research on gun-violence-related topics was severely curtailed; evidence regarding effects of gun violence on people and the economy was missing, and there was little research-backed evidence on the efficacy of particular policies. This is just beginning to change.

The 1996 Dickey Amendment barred the CDC from using funds in ways that could be used to advocate for gun control. Early in 2013, then-president Obama ordered the CDC and other "scientific agencies"

> to conduct or sponsor research into the causes of gun violence and the ways to prevent it. The Secretary shall begin by identifying the most pressing research questions with the greatest potential public health impact, and by assessing existing public health interventions being implemented across the Nation to prevent gun violence.
> -- Presidential Memorandum (1/16/13)

For years afterward, however, the CDC continued to avoid funding research that could be used in legislative arguments "intended to restrict or control the purchase or use of firearms." Only in 2021, with $25 million in federal funds earmarked for research on prevention of injury due to firearms, did the CDC began funding these inquiries again.

The result has been enormous knowledge gaps. CRDer Rachel Usdan is now executive director of Peace for DC, which seeks "to amplify and accelerate the efforts of DC's community gun violence prevention and intervention organizations." One of the new group's first efforts was to commission a study on the cost of gun violence – in health care, lost work, and many other factors, apart from loss of life and trauma to individuals.

Another "thunders ceased" situation grew from the summer of protests that ensued following the killing of George Floyd in May 2020. Sermons and statements were issued, services of mourning held, and then -- when more Black people were killed by police: nothing. Several Jews in CRD responded with "Dear Jews Who Say 'Black Lives Matter'" in Fall 2020:

Jews Who Say "Black Lives Matter"

In June of 2020, while protests were prevalent, hundreds of Jewish organizations, congregations, and clergy signed a statement of support for Black Lives. Matter. This was a big deal for many who had not previously uttered or signed onto those three words in order. Less than three months later, however, the same Jewish groups and leaders had nothing at all to say about MPD shooting a youth, just barely 18, to death on a District street. (Deon Kay was mentioned earlier, in Starting Points).

Despite promises less than three months old, organizations -- including 12 signatory synagogues inside DC, many others nearby, and plenty around the country who should have been concerned -- there was no Jewish call for accountability and transparency from government and from police.

We must remember, [from the "Jews for Black Lives" statement]:

When Black movements are undermined, it leads to more violence against Black people, including Black Jews (emphasis in original).

When Jewish institutions fail to support Black Lives Matter, or fall short in that effort, we contribute to the work of white supremacy, endangering Black and Jewish people, in our overlapping communities.

Missing Voices

The expression "*ha-kolot*," translated above as "the thunderings" or "the thunders," also means "the voices." Expanding the range of voices included in evidence we consider -- for any decision-making and in forming our world views -- is one function of cross-community dialogue.

The Official, Collective Shrug

The DC Council recently considered giving "surplus" land, at 2 Patterson NE, for what was proposed in 2019 as "NoMa's First Truly Mixed-Income Community, Centered Around The Arts & Culture." In exchange for land valued at millions, the developer would pay rent of $1 per year for 99 years (that's $99 for 99 years, no zeros missing) "as an incentive for the Developers to offer additional affordable units," beyond what is required when District-owned property is involved.

In 2021, DC's mayor asked the Council to approve land disposition, "following a community engagement process to obtain public input for the future use of the property." Mayor Murial Bowser wrote:

> The proposal will deliver a high-rise building with approximately 580 residential units ranging from studios to three- and four-bedrooms. The redevelopment of the Property will provide residential housing, communal spaces to enhance the atmosphere and sense of community for its residents, and will be a major step forward in the District's redevelopment.

The City's relatively new Council Office of Racial Equity (CORE) did as directed, analyzing this proposal and reporting its findings:

> A) the need for holistic reevaluation of public property surplus determinations. "As this case demonstrates, the Act's public hearing requirements do not guarantee meaningful participation by interested members of the public at the surplus consideration stage" (Committee chair's summary);

> B) "it is difficult to justify public land ever being deemed unnecessary for public use";

> C) this project would have no impact on racial equity in housing.

More specifically, CORE reports:

> Concerningly, the definition of "affordable" is race neutral and ignores large differences in Median Family Income across racial groups....but MFI and structural affordability challenges across racial groups are dramatically different.

> Concerningly, most planned units at 2 Patterson do not further the goals of the Comprehensive Plan* to build deeply affordable units for extremely low and very low income residents. Instead, the majority of "affordable units" (347) are set aside for those earning between 80 percent and 120 percent AMI....

Concerningly, original plans to develop the site and provide substantially more affordable housing were disregarded. According to testimony provided by the Executive, [other nearby projects would provide] all the necessary replacement housing and therefore, the property at 2 Patterson was released. To date, redevelopment of housing initiatives such as Temple Courts and Sursum Corda have displaced thousands of residents, been delayed for nearly two decades, and have failed to deliver on the promise of protecting five hundred twenty units of deeply subsidized housing and to also create six hundred new affordable units.**

Footnotes:

*Planning for 2 Patterson began before the final passage of the Comp Plan, which passed in 2021

**The Northwest One redevelopment plan was launched in 2005, which would have created 1,700 housing units including the one for one replacement of five hundred and twenty deeply subsidized units. In the Fall of 2020, the first phase of Northwest One finally broke ground.
--Full Racial Equity Impact Assessment at dcracialequity.org/

Image at left (FB post, 2013) is street festival at Sursum Corda housing cooperative housing, a few blocks from 2 Patterson NE and mentioned above as having been displaced. A few market tents, plus Black people of all ages, including one person assisting another up the curb, enjoying a summer day.

Although this project was originally advertised by the City as "Centered Around The Arts & Culture," renderings from KGD Architects (see right and below) display no discernible relationship to any art or culture of DC, and the two com-

mittee reports on this proposal include nothing about art or culture.

To recap -- giving the developer this land would

- provide affordable housing at a rate inconsistent with the City's goals,
- take no step toward racial equity in housing,
- fulfill no promise of new housing for already displaced communities,
- follow through on no art/culture vision.

The developer pays pocket change, while the District's official Council Office of Racial Equity warns that the project will squander a precious opportunity to reverse some of the long-standing wrongs in DC's land use.

The Council's response?

The Official Shrug:

"No problem. Maybe next time."

Council approval, with only two Councilmembers voting nay.

As with the images associated with MLK Gateway, renderings for 2 Patterson show a distinct absence of those currently in the area. Rendering below shows two-building highrise complex with street-level retail. Sidewalks are peopled with figures that look able-bodied, thin, and light-skinned. Rendering on previous page shows a closer view of street level building and courtyard with waterfall, fountain, and more thin, young, fit white people. Renderings are not neutral. This is the vision the City chose for this project on public land.

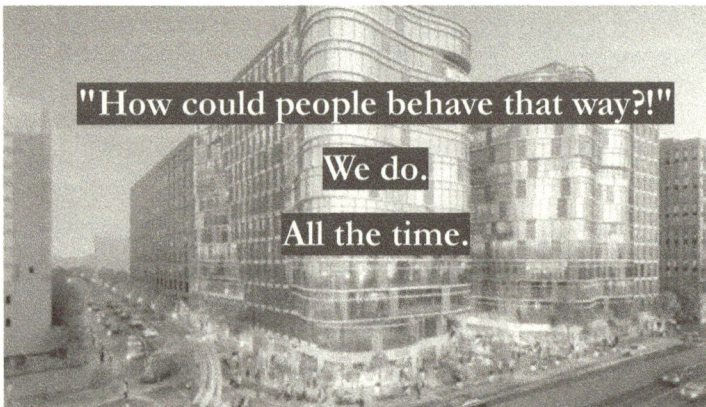

Rendering by KGD Architects of Monument Realty's plans for 2 Patterson

A Long Interval

"The length of time that the *Yisrael-ites* lived in *Mitzrayim* was four hundred and thirty years." -- Exodus 12:40

The specified length is explained in a variety of ways in Jewish teaching: numerology and symbolic readings, ancient numerical systems, various narrative approaches, and a range of interpretations of God's words to Abraham: "...your seed shall be strangers in a land not theirs, they shall be enslaved and oppressed for 400 years" (Gen 13:15).

A number of teachers insist that the meaning is, more simply: "a very long interval."

However, it is also useful to consider how numbers are written in biblical Hebrew: "thirty years and four hundred years." The phrasing can nudge us to consider those thirty years as both part of 430 and distinct from the other 400.

Three decades are long enough for art trends to develop and fashions to come and go, for businesses to flourish and fizzle, for whole regimes to rise and fall. A span of thirty years can see a human born and grow to adulthood, perhaps become a parent. While 400 years of oppression is in some ways abstract, many readers of this book will have personal experience of 30, maybe multiples of 30, years of oppression with consequent stresses and health threats.

In his *Bible Tales*, Dick Gregory (*z"l*) reflected on the Exodus story:

> Black people are herded into small, over-crowded areas called ghettos, made to live in substandard housing where heat, water, and plumbing facilities are lacking and adequate public services like garbage removal are withheld, making the ghetto areas breeding grounds for rats, disease, and death. Add to this the poor food found in ghetto supermarkets, the absence of health services, and the fires that consume the rundown houses and the little kids who live in them.
>
> The result is an infant mortality rate that is at least twice as high for Black folks as it is for white folks. a genocide plan a lot more subtle than Pharaoh's. -- *Dick Gregory's Bible Tales*, p.76-77

...Gregory's language dates this passage. We now have "areas of disinvestment" instead of "ghettos," for example, and "folks" is less common now than it was in the 1970s (although this author still uses it). But, otherwise, this passage is all too accurate today. In fact, we'll see in the next section that the disparity in infant mortality has actually increased since this writing....

Even if all these conditions had been eradicated as of this writing, however, the health effects for living people, and their children, would still be with us. And the fact that people reading this have lived with thirty years (and then some) of the conditions Gregory describes means that whole generations have lived, and some died, under the "millstone that is *Mitzrayim*." The effect of these particular decades is one weight, and the cumulative effect of the centuries is something else again:

> The length of time under the millstone that is *Mitzrayim* was thirty years and four hundred years (paraphrasing Exod 12:40).

Coming to an End?

The period of time that the *Yisrael-ites* had been in *Mitzrayim* is sometimes translated simply as the time they "lived there." But translators who seek to follow the Hebrew more closely use a noun for the "lived here" expression [מושב, *moshav* -- dwelling, situation]:

- "settlement" (both Robert Alter and Everett Fox, 20th Century US),

- "habitation" (Artscroll, 20th Century Ashkenazi Orthodox)

- "lifestyle" (*Me'am Lo'ez*, Ladino/Sephardic text, 18th Century Turkey).

The use of "lifestyle" for this passage is unusual and evocative. Here are two thoughts prompted by this translation:

A) The situation in *Mitzrayim* was, in some sense, a way of life for both *Mitzrayim-ites* and *Yisrael-ites;* and

B) Like all lifestyles, it will come to an end.

1	2	3	4	5	6	7
8	9	10	11	12	13	14
15	16	17	18	19	20	21
22	23	24	25	26	27	28
29	30	31	32	33	34	35
36	37	38	39	40	41	42
43	44	45	46	47	48	49

Recounting Exodus

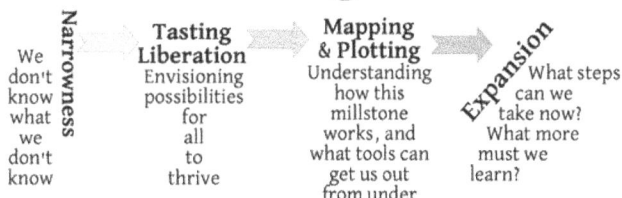

Narrowness → **Tasting Liberation** → **Mapping & Plotting** → **Expansion**

Narrowness	Tasting Liberation	Mapping & Plotting	Expansion
We don't know what we don't know	Envisioning possibilities for all to thrive	Understanding how this millstone works, and what tools can get us out from under	What steps can we take now? What more must we learn?

Where to Now?

At one point in the planning of this book, the idea was that we would first explore how oppression shows up in our lives and then move on to how we can respond. As it evolved, the journey did not end up on such an obviously hopeful note.

Still, there is great hope in beginning these explorations.

It's important to acknowledge how far we've traveled, how many questions we've asked, how many steps we've taken toward new visions of cross-community collaboration.... And how much more work is to be done.

The section on Response, Resistance, and Repair, ahead, just begins to suggest some ways forward.

"Response, Resistance, and Repair" begins on page 185.

To use the thought prompts without associated ritual, jump ahead to the prompts which begin on page 164.

For those seeking OMER COUNTING thoughts and rituals, see the next page for a related table of contents.

User-Defined Index

Counting Appendix

This section outlines a 49-stage journey to explore the workings of oppression and move toward Liberation. The journey can be undertaken in any way that works, in any timeframe. The series of thought-prompts need not be linked to Judaism or the Jewish calendar.

In addition, however, blessings and ritual counts are provided for those "Counting the Omer," from the second night of Passover through the eve of Shavuot.

Note: the commandment is to bless then count. So, we avoid telling someone who is observing *Sefira* the the current day's count, instead offering the previous day's count: E.g., "yesterday we counted four." This facilitates the right count once the blessing has been recited. This yesterday-focused practice can also offer another form of mindfulness for the journey, serving as a reminder that we are always arriving from where we've been.

Night and Day and the Whole Count

Also note that the Omer is counted at night. After sunset on the "old day," we name and look to the "new day." Counting can also be done on the following morning.

In addition, the commandment to count the Omer is understood as BOTH counting each day AND counting the entire period of seven weeks. So there are rules about what to do if a day is missed. I have been taught:
- we can catch up on one missed day, as soon as we remember;
- if we forget for two or more days, we can continue the count but no longer use the formal "blessing of mitzvah."

The logic for the latter is that we are no longer completing the full 49-day count and so not fulfilling that mitzvah.

The point of this particular journey is to learn something new, a little every day if possible, but there is no need to complete every day in order.

Counting Basics

"Counting the Omer" consists of three basic steps:

- Intention,
- Blessing, and, finally,
- Counting
- addition in some practices: Prayer/intention for captives

The opening words of intention in most prayerbooks are based on the biblical commandment, reminding the counter each day of the related biblical text. See "Biblical Intention." *Recounting Exodus* includes this and also offers additional intentions for this learning journey:

- an overall intention,
- a learning intention specific to the day's content, and
- an interpretive intention for the daily count.

Learning Focus

Overall intention:

> For this journey, from the first unknowing steps of freedom
> toward revelation and liberation for all,
> I undertake to know more today than I did yesterday
> about the workings of this millstone of oppression
> and how we might get ourselves, all of us, out from under under.

Launch for each day's thought:

> Here I am ready to _____ for this journey,
> undertaking to know more each day about the workings of oppression,
> so that we might get ourselves, all of us,
> out from under under this millstone that is the Narrow Place.

Interpretive blessing for the count:

Here I am, ready and prepared to fulfill this project of counting 49 days,
from Narrowness to Expansion,
seeking to examine oppression and envision liberation,
inspired by the Torah's counting of the Omer,
counting seven full weeks, from Liberation to Revelation,
until I reach fifty days,
and prepare to bring new thoughts before the Eternal and into the world.

Biblical Intention

The intention (Hebrew: *kavanah)* is, in many Jewish traditions, considered essential to focus the speech-act of counting. The *kavanah*/intention used in many Jewish traditions begins with an announcement of readiness. The basic statement, "Here I am, ready and prepared," incorporates in Hebrew, being a gendered language, assumptions about who is speaking. Many prayerbooks list only default, masculine language. Some include a feminine option as well. Only very recently has there been a non-binary option. (Visit nonbinaryHebrew.com for details.)

Here are the three current options, borrowed from Keshet: For LGBTQ Equality in Jewish Life, for the opening line. The text that follows, a direct quotation of Leviticus 23:15-16, is left unchanged.

Here I am, ready and prepared

[non-binary]   [feminine]   [masculine]

הִנְנִי מוּכָנֶה וּמְזֻמֶּנֶה   הִנְנִי מוּכָנָה וּמְזֻמֶּנֶת   הִנְנִי מוּכָן וּמְזֻמָּן

Hineni muchaneh um'zumeneh...   *Hineni muchanah um'zumenet...*   *Hineni muchan um'zuman...*

[All]

...לְקַיֵּם מִצְוַת עֲשֵׂה שֶׁל סְפִירַת הָעֹמֶר כְּמוֹ שֶׁכָּתוּב בַּתּוֹרָה

Ritual Focus

וּסְפַרְתֶּם לָכֶם מִמָּחֳרַת הַשַּׁבָּת
מִיּוֹם הֲבִיאֲכֶם אֶת עֹמֶר הַתְּנוּפָה
שֶׁבַע שַׁבָּתוֹת תְּמִימֹת תִּהְיֶינָה
עַד מִמָּחֳרַת הַשַּׁבָּת הַשְּׁבִיעִית תִּסְפְּרוּ חֲמִשִּׁים יוֹם
וְהִקְרַבְתֶּם מִנְחָה חֲדָשָׁה לַיי

...ləkayyem mitzvat aseh shel səfirat ha-omer, kəmo shekatuv batorah:
us'fartem lakhem mimacharat hashabbat,
miyom havi'akhem et omer hat'nufah,
sheva shabbatot temimot tih'yena,
ad mimacharat hashabbat hash'vi'it tis'pəru khamishim yom,
vəhikravtem minkha khadasha l'adonai.

... to fulfill the mitzvah of counting the Omer, as it is written in the Torah:
And you shall count for yourselves from the day after the Shabbat, from the day on which you bring the sheaf of the wave-offering, you shall count seven full weeks.
Until the day after the seventh Shabbat, you shall count fifty days, until you bring a new gift to the Eternal. (Leviticus 23:15-16)

In Hebrew, blessings incorporate divine gender, with masculine as default. Below are blessings with masculine and feminine God-language again from Keshet. Non-binary language is adapted from *Siddur Dvar Ḥadash*, put together by Brin Solomon (it/itself). "Voix" is an English alternative to use of (plural-sounding) "They" for God. More on this at inclusivesiddur.com.

Bless

Blessing with Masculine Language for God

בָּרוּךְ אַתָּה יי אֱלֹהֵינוּ מֶלֶךְ הָעוֹלָם
אֲשֶׁר קִדְּשָׁנוּ בְּמִצְוֹתָיו
וְצִוָּנוּ עַל סְפִירַת הָעֹמֶר

Barukh atah Adonai, Eloheinu melekh ha'olam
asher kidshanu bemitzvotav
v'tzivanu al sefirat ha'omer.

Blessed are You, Adonai, our God, ruler of the universe
who has made us holy with His commandments,
and commanded us to count the Omer.

Blessing with Feminine Language for God

בְּרוּכָה אַתְּ יָ-הּ אֱלֹהֵינוּ רוּחַ הָעוֹלָם
אֲשֶׁר קִדְּשָׁנוּ בְּמִצְוֹתָהּ
וְצִוָּנוּ עַל סְפִירַת הָעֹמֶר

Brukhah at Yah, ru'akh ha'olam
asher kidshanu bemitzvotah
v'tzivanu al sefirat ha'omer

Blessed are You, Yah, our God, spirit of the universe
who has made us holy with Her commandments,
and commanded us to count the Omer.

Blessing with Non-Binary Language for God

Brukheh ateh YHVH   בְּרוּכֶה אַתֶּה יהוה

Elohéinu ḥei ha'olamim   אֱלֹהֵינוּ חֵי הָעוֹלָמִים

asher kidshétnu   אֲשֶׁר קִדְּשֶׁתְנוּ

bəmitzvotéihe vətzivétnu   בְּמִצְוֹתֶיה וְצִוֶּתְנוּ

al sefirat ha'omer   עַל סְפִירַת הָעֹמֶר

Blessed are you, YHVH,
our God, Life of endless worlds,
who made us holy
with Voix commandments and commanded us
to count the Omer.

Count

The Bible mentions counting 49 days and counting seven weeks. These are considered separate commandments, so we mention both days and weeks in each day's count. As mentioned previously, the commandment is to bless then count. So, we avoid telling someone who is observing *Sefira* the the current day's count, instead prompting them with yesterday's count.

Count

הַיּוֹם_____ יוֹם שֶׁהֵם _____ שָׁבוּעוֹת וְ_____ יָמִים לָעֹמֶר

Hayom _____ shehem
____ shavuot v'____ yamim laomer.

Today is _____ which is
_____weeks and _____days of the Omer.

Final intention/prayer

Those so moved add something like, "In the spirit of the Exodus, I set an intention (pray) for release of all whose bodies and spirits remain captive," along with any thoughts/prayers/actions to support release of captives.

To recap: Focus, Bless, Count (and Pray)

1) Intention: Biblical Intention in Hebrew and/or English AND/OR Recounting Exodus version (English-only).

2) Blessing: in Hebrew and/or English, choosing one of the forms of address for God above or making up your own

3) Count days and weeks in Hebrew and/or English.

4) If so moved, add a prayer or intention for captives. (English -only as provided here -- some add Psalms or other prayers in Hebrew.)

Forty-Nine Thought-Prompts/Omer Count

It Begins.

Name one change that you believe necessary but many around you see no urgency to address. What factors fuel your sense of urgency? What factors seem to influence others' comfort with the current situation? Might that change with a different perspective?

Name one change that others around you are demanding but you do not feel drawn to address. What factors fuel their urgency? What factors influence your comfort with the current situation? Might that change with a different perspective?

[Intention, Blessing, Count]

הַיּוֹם שְׁנֵי יָמִים לָעֹמֶר *Hayom yom echad la-omer.*
Today is one day of the Omer.

We counted 1.

Were we taught to consider either *Yisrael* or *Mitzrayim* "our people"?
If so, how do we relate to the other group?

Do we identify with attachment to home and feelings about building community with newcomers? And/or do we identify with feelings about leaving home and hopes for a better future?

Do we sympathize more with a group of 70 seeking refuge, as *Yisrael* and family are introduced here, than with the large population we will meet in just a few verses? Why? Do our sympathies change with the state's labeling: welcome workers, economic threat, or potential enemy/fifth column?

How do we imagine these groups in terms of family structure, ethnic background, sexuality, wealth and other factors? Are they like or unlike us?

Can we explain, for ourselves and others, how our background influences our perspectives on what is happening in the opening verse of Exodus?...or anywhere in the world?

[Intention, Blessing, Count]

הַיּוֹם שְׁנֵי יָמִים לָעֹמֶר *Hayom sh'nei yamim la-omer.*
Today is two days of the Omer

2

We counted 2.

Consider reports violence, especially killings by police officers. Compare reports from your own town or look at 18-year-old Deon Kay killed by DC's police (9/2/20): Do we begin with MPD's report of a justified fatal shot? With earlier actions of the officers and/or Deon? the DC Auditor's report on the officers' "entirely improvised" and "reckless" approach? with Kelly Brown Douglas's *Stand Your Ground: Black Bodies and the Justice of God*?

Consider reports of the Colleyville, TX incident. Do we start with sources outside, saying "hostages rescued"? with inside accounts of an escape sans external intervention? with R' Charlie Cytron-Walker's welcoming a cold stranger? with R' Angela Buchdahl, one of the country's most prominent rabbis of color, and how the alleged perpetrator came to think her in charge of what he wanted? with the individual who admits to selling a stolen, semiautomatic weapon? or with a judicial system that can make this Black man the face of a hate crime/act of terrorism that he did not commit?

[Intention, Blessing, Count]

הַיּוֹם שְׁלֹשָׁה יָמִים לָעֹמֶר *Hayom sh'loshah yamim la-omer.*
Today is three days of he Omer

3

We counted 3.

With a view to "getting out" --
-- what Narrow Place are you, personally, attempting to escape this year?
-- what Narrow Place does your community need to leave behind?

Considering a "better place" --
-- do you have a destination in mind, as you leave the Narrow Place?
-- what do you envision, at the end of the road, for your community?

On this journey --
-- is there something essential to be learned from the wilderness itself?
-- how might your community benefit from accepting that some things have been left behind, while the destination is still out of sight?

Does one view of Exodus from oppression seem more apt than another, for you personally and for your community?

[Intention, Blessing, Count]

הַיּוֹם אַרְבָּעָה יָמִים לָעֹמֶר *Hayom arbaah yamim la-omer.*
Today is four days of the Omer

4

We counted 4.

Has the Exodus/Passover story experienced something of a "crash" for you? for your community? At the very least, we must ask some tough questions, of ourselves and our communities, about this concept of "joining together and marching":

Are we prepared to head toward something **truly different**?

Will we **let go of what we have** in order to get there?

With whom have we **joined hands**? Whom have we **left behind**?

Have we been marching toward a liberation -- that never seems to materialize -- for so long that we now wonder if it's **worth the upheaval**?

[Intention, Blessing, Count]

הַיּוֹם חֲמִשָּׁה יָמִים לָעֹמֶר

Hayom chamishah yamim la-omer.
Today is five days of the omer.

5

We counted 5.

Can anyone be brought out "from under the millstone that is [*Mitzrayim*]" while they themselves remain unmoved?

Is rescue possible for those who remain chained to old ideas, accepting enslavement, for themselves or others, as due course?

Can anyone be redeemed "with an outstretched arm and formidable judgments" without experiencing disruption to life as usual?

Can a Liberation experience have an impact for us or for anyone else, if nothing changes in our commitments?

[Intention, Blessing, Count]

הַיּוֹם שִׁשָּׁה יָמִים לָעֹמֶר
Hayom shishah yamim la-omer.
Today is six days of the Omer.

6

We counted 6.

Are those not actively suffering from oppression allowed to decide what the times will bear in terms of community change? How can this reality be highlighted so as to encourage a change of perspective?

Have you heard these themes directed at you or others?
"You're too young to know" and/or "You're too old to understand."
"Now is not the time...Be patient." or "You'll get us all killed."
"We are better off with the devil we know."
What kinds of responses have been tried? What might work better?

And what about these old bones? Are we honoring ancestors by carrying them? Or are we tied to older visions and promises that are holding us back, might even shame those same ancestors? What does it mean for a community to be obligated? at all? What do we owe leaders, other community members, or vows of the past?

[Intention, Blessing, Count]

הַיּוֹם שִׁבְעָה יָמִים שֶׁהֵם שָׁבוּעַ אֶחָד לָעֹמֶר

Hayom shivah yamim shehem shavua echad la-omer.
Today is seven days which is one week of the Omer.

7

We counted 7.

How are we, like the midwives at the start of the story (Ex 1:15-21), attempting to stand up to power and for life?

How are we, like Moses (Ex 2ff), struggling with identity -- raised in one household and culture but connected in many ways to another?

How are we, like Pharaoh (Ex 1ff), impatient with the past and fearful of the future, ready to knock down anyone or anything that threatens those we believe we must protect?

As *Yisrael-ites* or *Mitzrayim-ites*, what assumptions and experiences form our views?

Can we learn to hold more than one point of view at the same time or in conversation with one another?

[Intention, Blessing, Count]

הַיּוֹם שְׁמוֹנָה יָמִים שֶׁהֵם שָׁבוּעַ אֶחָד וְיוֹם אֶחָד לָעֹמֶר

Hayom sh'monah yamim shehem shavua echad v'yom echad la-omer.
Today is eight days, which is one week and one day of the Omer.

We counted 8.

Non-Black Jews might have experiences of oppression and carry generational trauma. We can learn from others. But that does not make us first-hand experts on topics like "America's treatment of Black folks."

Non-Jewish folks might have experiences of oppression, carry generational trauma, and can learn from Jews. But non-Jews are not first-hand experts on topics like "alarm bells that anti-Jewish conspiracy raise for me."

How do we speak and write so as to distinguish shared, or universal, experiences from more particular ones?

[Intention, Blessing, Count]

הַיּוֹם תִּשְׁעָה יָמִים שֶׁהֵם שָׁבוּעַ אֶחָד וּשְׁנֵי יָמִים לָעֹמֶר

Hayom tishah yamim shehem shavua echad ushnei yamim la-omer.

Today is nine days, which is one week and two days of he Omer.

We counted 9.

Rabbi Gerry Serotta says that, instead of focusing on the identities of the people who left, we should instead ask:

> What was it that compelled some people to leave behind the Narrow Place and seek liberation outside of the circumstances they previously knew? How can we emulate THAT?

[Intention, Blessing, Count]

הַיּוֹם עֲשָׂרָה יָמִים שֶׁהֵם שָׁבוּעַ אֶחָד וּשְׁלֹשָׁה יָמִים לָעֹמֶר

Hayom asarah yamim
shehem shavua echad ushloshah yamim la-omer.

Today is ten days, which is one week and three days of the Omer.

We counted 10.

R' Jacob argues that existing personal friendships were changed through propaganda. **Might a counter-effort** have helped them survive?

History has shown us individual friendships surviving, and serving to ameliorate effects of oppressive conditions around the globe, for short periods.

What about the long-haul? At what point does friendship become untenable if the systemic conditions are not addressed?

Consider the role of "systematically encouraged hate" in our lives today.

How has it affected relationships between community groups?

How has it affected your personal relationships?

[Intention, Blessing, Count]

הַיּוֹם אַחַד עָשָׂר יוֹם שֶׁהֵם שָׁבוּעַ אֶחָד וְאַרְבָּעָה יָמִים לָעֹמֶר

Hayom achad asar yom
shehem shavua echad v'arbaah yamim la-omer.

Today is eleven days, which is one week and four days of the Omer.

11

We counted 11.

Can a single relationship -- or even a bunch of them -- influence the kind of endemic hate suggested here?

Can a single relationship -- between particular political or community leaders, for example -- help to control hate-based behaviors?

What impact can individual relationships have on systemic oppression?

Meanwhile, what it is the cost of maintaining those relationships?

[Intention, Blessing, Count]

הַיּוֹם שְׁנֵים עָשָׂר יוֹם שֶׁהֵם שָׁבוּעַ אֶחָד וַחֲמִשָּׁה יָמִים לָעֹמֶר

Hayom sh'neim asar yom
shehem shavua echad vachamishah yamim la-omer.

Today is twelve days, which is one week and five days of the Omer.

12

We counted 12.

Beyond optics, can one relationship promote intergroup understanding?

What about those optics: Do they help in a crisis? for the long haul?

Why do these outsized roles exist? Are we victims of opportunists, or do we give Big Names space so they can tread where we'd rather not?

Do Big Names represent us (even while benefiting from the spotlight)?

[Intention, Blessing, Count]

הַיּוֹם שְׁלֹשָׁה עָשָׂר יוֹם שֶׁהֵם שָׁבוּעַ אֶחָד וְשִׁשָּׁה יָמִים לָעֹמֶר

Hayom sh'loshah asar yom
shehem shavua echad v'shishah yamim la-omer.

Today is thirteen days, which is one week and six days of the Omer.

13

We counted 13.

Identify an experience in which you engaged in a group from a position of less power or minority status: newcomer in a long-standing group, non-Zionist in a mainstream synagogue, lower income in a well-off group, etc.

Identify an experience in which you engaged in a group from a position of more power or majority status.

Compare the effort involved in each. (More on this next week.)

[Intention, Blessing, Count]

הַיּוֹם אַרְבָּעָה עָשָׂר יוֹם שֶׁהֵם שְׁנֵי שָׁבוּעוֹת לָעְׂמֶר

Hayom arbaah asar yom shehem sh'nei shavuot la-omer.

Today is fourteen days, which is two weeks of the Omer.

14

We counted 14.

When do you go along to get along in civic, religious, and other groups?

When do you insist on being recognized, being allowed to fully show up?

Does your decision depend on speaking for yourself vs. for a group?

[Intention, Blessing, Count]

הַיּוֹם חֲמִשָּׁה עָשָׂר יוֹם שֶׁהֵם שְׁנֵי שָׁבוּעוֹת וְיוֹם אֶחָד לָעְׂמֶר

Hayom chamishah asar yom
shehem sh'nei shavuot v'yom echad la-omer.

Today is fifteen days, which is two weeks and one day of the Omer.

15

We counted 15.

Have you been asked, "Why are you here?" "Did someone invite you?" upon arrival at your place of worship or other gathering spot?

Are you regularly assumed, by strangers, to belong in Jewish spaces? Do you feel welcome and safe when facing security guards/"greeters"?

Has your worship community discussed the impact of such a presence on members, visitors, and others in the neighborhood?

[Intention, Blessing, Count]

הַיּוֹם שִׁשָּׁה עָשָׂר יוֹם שֶׁהֵם שְׁנֵי שָׁבוּעוֹת וּשְׁנֵי יָמִים לָעֹמֶר.

Hayom shishah asar yom
shehem sh'nei shavuot ushnei yamim la-omer.

Today is sixteen days, which is two weeks and two days of the Omer.

16

We counted 16.

Based on your historical recollections, have Jewish communities that were careful "not to grow too distant from the society" around them faced less anti-Jewish sentiment and behavior in the long run?

How does engagement "work" in the analysis below (more on this later), from *Understanding Antisemitism: An Offering to Our Movement*:

> The oppression of Jews is a conjuring trick... a set up that works through misdirection, that uses privilege to hide the gears...a minority of us, are offered the uncertain bribes of privilege and protection. Privilege for a visible sample of us is the only way to make the whole tricky business work.... -- Aurora Levins Morales

Does intergroup interaction prevent dehumanization or exploitation?

[Intention, Blessing, Count]

הַיּוֹם שִׁבְעָה עָשָׂר יוֹם שֶׁהֵם שְׁנֵי שָׁבוּעוֹת וּשְׁלֹשָׁה יָמִים לָעֹמֶר

Hayom shivah asar yom
shehem sh'nei shavuot ushloshah yamim la-omer.
Today is seventeen days,
which is two weeks and three days of the Omer.

----

17 We counted 17.

Can empathy and action be stirred through "putting a face" on statistics?

Can we understand a wider problem through one "human face" alone?

[Intention, Blessing, Count]

הַיּוֹם שְׁמוֹנָה עָשָׂר יוֹם שֶׁהֵם שְׁנֵי שָׁבוּעוֹת וְאַרְבָּעָה יָמִים לָעֹמֶר

Hayom sh'monah asar yom
shehem sh'nei shavuot v'arbaah yamim la-omer.
Today is eighteen days, which is two weeks and four days of the Omer.

18

We counted 18.

How do spiritual communities effectively address mourning for regular losses and on-going grief experienced by only one part of the community -- or, perhaps, by neighbors who are not part of the worship community?

Should the focus be on mourning alone or mourning-that leads to action?

[Intention, Blessing, Count]

הַיּוֹם תִּשְׁעָה עָשָׂר יוֹם שֶׁהֵם שְׁנֵי שָׁבוּעוֹת וַחֲמִשָּׁה יָמִים לָעֹמֶר.

Hayom tishah asar yom
shehem sh'nei shavuot vachamishah yamim la-omer.
Today is nineteen days, which is two weeks and five days of the Omer.

19

We counted 19.

What is the value and span of such bridges? Who benefits? Do we know?

[Intention, Blessing, Count]

הַיּוֹם עֶשְׂרִים יוֹם שֶׁהֵם שְׁנֵי שָׁבוּעוֹת וְשִׁשָּׁה יָמִים לָעֹמֶר.

Hayom esrim yom shehem sh'nei shavuot v'shishah yamim la-omer.
Today is twenty days, which is two weeks and six days of the Omer.

20

We counted 20.

If we do not grieve, what are we?
If we cannot grieve and still act, who will?

[Intention, Blessing, Count]

הַיּוֹם אֶחָד וְעֶשְׂרִים יוֹם שֶׁהֵם שְׁלֹשָׁה שָׁבוּעוֹת לָעֹמֶר

Hayom echad v'esrim yom shehem sh'loshah shavuot la-omer
Today is twenty-one days, which is three weeks of the Omer

21

We counted 21.

How do we tell the stories of movements and their interactions

How do we remember individuals within movements?

Might remembering differently mean going forward differently?

[Intention, Blessing, Count]

הַיּוֹם שְׁנַיִם וְעֶשְׂרִים יוֹם שֶׁהֵם שְׁלֹשָׁה שָׁבוּעוֹת וְיוֹם אֶחָד לָעְמֶר

Hayom sh'nayim v'esrim yom
shehem sh'loshah shavuot v'yom echad la-omer.
Today is twenty-two days,
which is three weeks and one day to the Omer.

22

We counted 22.

Have key teachings lost context, making idols of moments of change?

Might we more profitably recall AJH, weeks prior to the iconic moment, leading a group to FBI HQ in NYC to protest Bloody Sunday and call for arrest of rioting police (thus landing himself on the FBI watch list)?

[Intention, Blessing, Count]

הַיּוֹם שְׁלֹשָׁה וְעֶשְׂרִים יוֹם שֶׁהֵם שְׁלֹשָׁה שָׁבוּעוֹת וּשְׁנֵי יָמִים לָעְמֶר

Hayom sh'loshah v'esrim yom
shehem sh'loshah shavuot ushnei yamim la-omer.
Today is twenty-three days,
which is three weeks and two days of the Omer.

Recounting Exodus

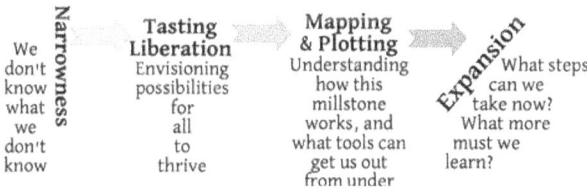

Narrowness	Tasting Liberation	Mapping & Plotting	Expansion
We don't know what we don't know	Envisioning possibilities for all to thrive	Understanding how this millstone works, and what tools can get us out from under	What steps can we take now? What more must we learn?

23

We counted 23.

How often do we allow our communities, Jewish and not, to claim we "have always" supported MLK, when history says otherwise?

How often does our view of MLK leave out criticism -- from in- and outside his own community -- as well as complex interactions with other Black leaders, various Christian groups, and a host of other sources?

Do we consider the biblical Joseph's likely detractors, within the larger family of Jacob as well as in other parts of *Mitzrayim-ite* society? The text is not explicit, but guarding and remembering Joseph's whole legacy, like MLK's, as an example of intergroup relations in is not a simple matter.

[Intention, Blessing, Count]

הַיּוֹם אַרְבָּעָה וְעֶשְׂרִים יוֹם שֶׁהֵם שְׁלֹשָׁה שָׁבוּעוֹת וּשְׁלֹשָׁה יָמִים לָעֹמֶר

*Hayom arbaah v'esrim yom
shehem sh'loshah shavuot ushloshah yamim la-omer.*
Today is twenty-four days,
which is three weeks and three days of the Omer.

24

We counted 24.

Review some national background, e.g., "whiteness" as a legal property.

Consider some structures constructed through labor of enslaved and oppressed people -- the White House, the transcontinental railway, the university down the road or maybe where you studied, e.g.

Discover/recall some hyperlocal background: Who owned the house on the corner in previous generations, and what restaurants have come and gone before your favorite arrived?

[Intention, Blessing, Count]

הַיּוֹם חֲמִשָּׁה וְעֶשְׂרִים יוֹם שֶׁהֵם שְׁלֹשָׁה שָׁבוּעוֹת וְאַרְבָּעָה יָמִים לָעֹמֶר

*Hayom chamishah v'esrim yom
shehem sh'loshah shavuot v'arbaah yamim la-omer.*
Today is twenty-five days,
which is three weeks and four days of the Omer.

----

25 **We counted 25.**

Does a newcomer have an obligation to learn a place's history?

Who gets to define the culture of a place with disparate residents?

[Intention, Blessing, Count]

הַיּוֹם שִׁשָּׁה וְעֶשְׂרִים יוֹם שֶׁהֵם שְׁלשָׁה שָׁבוּעוֹת וַחֲמִשָּׁה יָמִים לָעֹמֶר
*Hayom shishah v'esrim yom
shehem sh'loshah shavuot vachamishah yamim la-omer.*
Today is twenty-six days,
which is three weeks and five days of the Omer.

We counted 26 **26**

Do we recognize multiple paths bringing varied communities into one spot and notice how those paths have been intertwined?

Do we notice how it all takes place in relation to an overarching power?

Do we understand the long-term consequences of relating to that power?

[Intention, Blessing, Count]

הַיּוֹם שִׁבְעָה וְעֶשְׂרִים יוֹם שֶׁהֵם שְׁלשָׁה שָׁבוּעוֹת וְשִׁשָּׁה יָמִים לָעֹמֶר
*Hayom shivah v'esrim yom
shehem sh'loshah shavuot v'shishah yamim la-omer.*
Today is twenty-seven days,
which is three weeks and six days of the Omer.

----

27 **We counted 27.**

Doesn't much depend on how we read "the people"?

Clearly R' David, like much of Jewish commentary, focuses on *Yisrael-ite* suffering; but that's not the whole picture.

Can we re-tell the story to include how everyone suffered or thrived?

[Intention, Blessing, Count]

הַיּוֹם שְׁמוֹנָה וְעֶשְׂרִים יוֹם שֶׁהֵם אַרְבָּעָה שָׁבוּעוֹת לָעֹמֶר
Hayom sh'monah v'esrim yom shehem arbaah shavuot la-omer.
Today is twenty-eight days, which is four weeks of the Omer.

28

We counted 28.

Who, today, is trying to govern from a place of "dread"?

Which public conversations are driven by this concept?

How are attempts to avoid "dread" in one form or another fueling our housing, education, and other budget decisions?

[Intention, Blessing, Count]

הַיּוֹם תִּשְׁעָה וְעֶשְׂרִים יוֹם שֶׁהֵם אַרְבָּעָה שָׁבוּעוֹת וְיוֹם אֶחָד לָעֹמֶר

Hayom tishah v'esrim yom
shehem arbaah shavuot v'yom echad la-omer.
Today is twenty-nine days,
which is four weeks and one day of the Omer.

We counted 29. 　29

Look at local and/or national treatment of Black people from the lens of these Exodus verses. Do you see attempts to "deal shrewdly"?

[Intention, Blessing, Count]

הַיּוֹם שְׁלֹשִׁים יוֹם שֶׁהֵם אַרְבָּעָה שָׁבוּעוֹת וּשְׁנֵי יָמִים לָעֹמֶר

Hayom sh'loshim yom shehem arbaah shavuot ushnei yamim la-omer.
Today is thirty days, which is four weeks and two days of the Omer.

30　We counted 30.

Does dread work differently in racism and anti-Jewishness? in fear of Others linked to economic and immigration concerns? in homophobia?

[Intention, Blessing, Count]

הַיּוֹם אֶחָד וּשְׁלֹשִׁים יוֹם שֶׁהֵם אַרְבָּעָה שָׁבוּעוֹת וּשְׁלֹשָׁה יָמִים לָעֹמֶר

Hayom echad ushloshim yom
shehem arbaah shavuot ushloshah yamim la-omer.
Today is thirty-one days,
which is four weeks and three days of the Omer.

31

We counted 31.

Like Pharaoh, do we -- as individuals and in political groups -- envision others "joining enemies" against us?

If we respond like Pharaoh, who, ultimately, gets hurt?

[Intention, Blessing, Count]

הַיּוֹם שְׁנַיִם וּשְׁלֹשִׁים יוֹם שֶׁהֵם אַרְבָּעָה שָׁבוּעוֹת וְאַרְבָּעָה יָמִים לָעֹמֶר
Hayom sh'nayim ushloshim yom
shehem arbaah shavuot v'arbaah yamim la-omer.
Today is thirty-two days,
which is four weeks and four days of the Omer.

32

We counted 32.

Do we give the erroneous impression that all is well in personal and/or communal relationships while harboring inner disrespect?

What, if any, role can intergroup dialogue play in addressing this?

[Intention, Blessing, Count]

הַיּוֹם שְׁלֹשָׁה וּשְׁלֹשִׁים יוֹם שֶׁהֵם אַרְבָּעָה שָׁבוּעוֹת וַחֲמִשָּׁה יָמִים לָעֹמֶר
Hayom sh'loshah ushloshim yom
shehem arbaah shavuot vachamishah yamim la-omer.
Today is thirty-three days,
which is four weeks and five days of the Omer.

33

We counted 33.

Can intergroup dialogue serve as a model for respect?

What factors are important in giving and receiving respect?

[Intention, Blessing, Count]

הַיּוֹם אַרְבָּעָה וּשְׁלֹשִׁים יוֹם שֶׁהֵם אַרְבָּעָה שָׁבוּעוֹת וְשִׁשָּׁה יָמִים לָעֹמֶר
Hayom arbaah ushloshim yom
shehem arbaah shavuot v'shishah yamim la-omer.
Today is thirty-four days, which is four weeks and six days of the Omer.

We counted 34. 34

How do we foster true relationship and trust across disparate groups?

How do we ensure that innocence or worth are never up for debate?

[Intention, Blessing, Count]

הַיּוֹם חֲמִשָּׁה וּשְׁלֹשִׁים יוֹם שֶׁהֵם חֲמִשָּׁה שָׁבוּעוֹת לָעֹמֶר
Hayom chamishah ushloshim yom
shehem chamishah shavuot la-omer.
Today is thirty-five days, which is five weeks of the Omer.

----

35 We counted 35.

How do considerations around "the event of war" relate to the topics of trust and worth raised in the previous stage of the journey?

How do your own experiences, assumptions, and privileges influence your perspective on how close or distant the US is to "the event of war"?

[Intention, Blessing, Count]

הַיּוֹם שִׁשָּׁה וּשְׁלֹשִׁים יוֹם שֶׁהֵם חֲמִשָּׁה שָׁבוּעוֹת וְיוֹם אֶחָד לָעֹמֶר
Hayom shishah ushloshim yom
shehem chamishah shavuot v'yom echad la-omer.
Today is thirty-six days, which is five weeks and one day of the Omer.

----

36 We counted 36.

How is DC/Washington sold for business and residence these days?

Who benefits? Who ends up displaced?

What sold you on your current place of residence?

[Intention, Blessing, Count]

הַיּוֹם שִׁבְעָה וּשְׁלֹשִׁים יוֹם שֶׁהֵם חֲמִשָּׁה שָׁבוּעוֹת וּשְׁנֵי יָמִים לָעֹמֶר
Hayom shivah ushloshim yom
shehem chamishah shavuot ushnei yamim la-omer.
Today is thirty-seven days,
which is five weeks and two days of the Omer.

37

We counted 37.

Who convinced potential residents that the area was "hip"?

How do long-time residents and formerly-enslaved people fit into the story of the new, hip Pitom?

What kind of stories about the not-so-hip, old Pitom helped pave the way for the new?

Also, how long did developers let properties sit, waiting for the day they could cash in, instead of contributing to the vibrancy of Pitom all along?

[Intention, Blessing, Count]

הַיּוֹם שְׁמוֹנָה וּשְׁלֹשִׁים יוֹם שֶׁהֵם חֲמִשָּׁה שָׁבוּעוֹת וּשְׁלֹשָׁה יָמִים לָעֹמֶר

Hayom sh'monah ushloshim yom
shehem chamishah shavuot ushloshah yamim la-omer.
Today is thirty-eight days,
which is five weeks and three days of the Omer.

38

We counted 38.

Consider the numbers: 80,000 Black residents lost in twenty years. The percentage of Black residents dropping by half in fifty years.

Is this "just" a result of market forces?

[Intention, Blessing, Count]

הַיּוֹם תִּשְׁעָה וּשְׁלֹשִׁים יוֹם שֶׁהֵם חֲמִשָּׁה שָׁבוּעוֹת וְאַרְבָּעָה יָמִים לָעֹמֶר

Hayom tishah ushloshim yom
shehem chamishah shavuot v'arbaah yamim la-omer.
Today is thirty-nine days,
which is five weeks and four days of the Omer.

39

We counted 39.

Even those who do not live and/or work in DC should know something about land use and its effects on the population in the nation's capital.

Wherever you do live and work, there are land use and displacement stories, and their results, that you should know.

[Intention, Blessing, Count]

הַיּוֹם אַרְבָּעִים יוֹם שֶׁהֵם חֲמִשָּׁה שָׁבוּעוֹת וַחֲמִשָּׁה יָמִים לָעֹמֶר

Hayom arbaim yom
shehem chamishah shavuot vachamishah yamim la-omer.
Today is forty days, which is five weeks and five days of the Omer.

40

We counted 40.

Is encouraging low-rent, funkier businesses when times are hard, then pushing them out when values go up, an example of not-knowing-Joseph "moral deficiency" discussed in Day 25? If so, how can it be prevented?

[Intention, Blessing, Count]

הַיּוֹם אֶחָד וְאַרְבָּעִים יוֹם שֶׁהֵם חֲמִשָּׁה שָׁבוּעוֹת וְשִׁשָּׁה יָמִים לָעֹמֶר
Hayom echad v'arbaim yom
shehem chamishah shavuot v'shishah yamim la-omer.
Today is forty-one days, which is five weeks and six days of the Omer.

41

We counted 41.

What are the predictable, but not immediate, results of wholesale displacement of people, in DC and other locales?

What happens, in the the long run, to communities whose businesses are regularly destroyed in pursuit of greater profits?

[Intention, Blessing, Count]

הַיּוֹם שְׁנַיִם וְאַרְבָּעִים יוֹם שֶׁהֵם שִׁשָּׁה שָׁבוּעוֹת לָעֹמֶר
Hayom sh'nayim v'arbaim yom shehem shishah shavuot la-omer.
Today is forty-two days, which is six weeks of the Omer.

----

42 We counted 42.

How are you supporting healthier outcomes for Black mothers and babies right now?

Learn about and support the Black Mamas Matter Alliance.

If you can offer material support, find an organization local to you and/or support Mamatoto Village in DC.

[Intention, Blessing, Count]

הַיּוֹם שְׁלֹשָׁה וְאַרְבָּעִים יוֹם שֶׁהֵם שִׁשָּׁה שָׁבוּעוֹת וְיוֹם אֶחָד לָעֹמֶר
Hayom sh'loshah v'arbaim yom
shehem shishah shavuot v'yom echad la-omer
Today is forty-three days, which is six weeks and one day of the Omer

----

We counted 43. **43**

Where are the Level I or II trauma centers near you? (If you live in a rural area or certain parts of some cities, it can be quite a distance.)

What kind of arrangements are available for transporting stabilized patients who must be moved from a Level III or IV center, if there is one, to a facility with more resources?

Who makes the decisions about resource distribution?

How can planning decisions be influenced?

[Intention, Blessing, Count]

הַיּוֹם אַרְבָּעָה וְאַרְבָּעִים יוֹם שֶׁהֵם שִׁשָּׁה שָׁבוּעוֹת וּשְׁנֵי יָמִים לָעֹמֶר
Hayom arbaah v'arbaim yom
shehem shishah shavuot ushnei yamim la-omer.
Today is forty-four days, which is six weeks and two days of the Omer.

----

44 We counted 44.

Do we allow legislative and budget decisions to be made based on only whose households have been immediately affected?

Is the solution to change the households represented?

Is there a way to expand concern to households we might not know?

[Intention, Blessing, Count]

הַיּוֹם חֲמִשָּׁה וְאַרְבָּעִים יוֹם שֶׁהֵם שִׁשָּׁה שָׁבוּעוֹת וּשְׁלֹשָׁה יָמִים לָעֹמֶר
Hayom chamishah v'arbaim yom
shehem shishah shavuot ushloshah yamim la-omer.
Today is forty-five days, which is six weeks and three days of the Omer.

45

We counted 45.

Learn about and support the T.R.I.G.G.E.R (The Reason I Grabbed a Gun Evolved from Risk) Project.

[Intention, Blessing, Count]

הַיּוֹם שִׁשָּׁה וְאַרְבָּעִים יוֹם שֶׁהֵם שִׁשָּׁה שָׁבוּעוֹת וְאַרְבָּעָה יָמִים לָעֹמֶר
Hayom shishah v'arbaim yom
shehem shishah shavuot v'arbaah yamim la-omer.
Today is forty-six days, which is six weeks and four days of the Omer.

46

We counted 46.

Can we share evidence of the need for change, in so many areas -- locally, nationally, globally -- without exhausting ourselves and others?

Should we specialize, limit our focus? **Whom do we trust** to direct decision-making if we cannot follow all the evidence ourselves?

[Intention, Blessing, Count]

הַיּוֹם שִׁבְעָה וְאַרְבָּעִים יוֹם שֶׁהֵם שִׁשָּׁה שָׁבוּעוֹת וַחֲמִשָּׁה יָמִים לָעֹמֶר
Hayom shivah v'arbaim yom
shehem shishah shavuot vachamishah yamim la-omer.
Today is forty-seven days,
which is six weeks and five days of the Omer.

Are we there yet?

Recounting Exodus

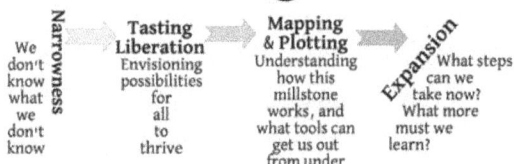

Narrowness
We don't know what we don't know → Tasting Liberation: Envisioning possibilities for all to thrive → Mapping & Plotting: Understanding how this millstone works, and what tools can get us out from under → Expansion: What steps can we take now? What more must we learn?

47

We counted 47.

As we plod along towards one destination, what have we learned that will serve us on the next legs of this journey?

What new ideas or commitments have we grown that we can now reap?

[Intention, Blessing, Count]

הַיּוֹם שְׁמוֹנָה וְאַרְבָּעִים יוֹם שֶׁהֵם שִׁשָּׁה שָׁבוּעוֹת וְשִׁשָּׁה יָמִים לָעֹמֶר

Hayom sh'monah v'arbaim yom
shehem shishah shavuot v'shishah yamim la-omer.
Today is forty-eight days, which is six weeks and six days of the Omer.

48

We counted 48.

At Passover, we leave *Mitzrayim* before knowing much about what's ahead.
After weeks of journey, are we clearer about what needs to change?
Approaching Sinai, are we ready to learn what must end?

[Intention, Blessing, Count]

הַיּוֹם תִּשְׁעָה וְאַרְבָּעִים יוֹם שֶׁהֵם שִׁבְעָה שָׁבוּעוֹת לָעֹמֶר

Hayom tishah v'arbaim yom shehem shivah shavuot la-omer
Today is forty-nine days, which is seven weeks of the Omer

Response, Resistance, Repair, Rescue

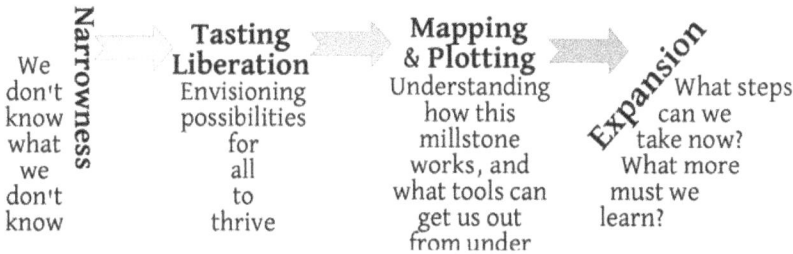

After a respite, at the close of 49 stages/days, it's time to put whatever we've learned so far into action. And to aid in that process and suggest more hope ahead, here are a few further stages.

The number 50 belongs to the festival pause.

The rest of these stages are numbered "51," an important number for DC...

Recounting Exodus

Narrowness	Tasting Liberation	Mapping & Plotting	Expansion
We don't know what we don't know	Envisioning possibilities for all to thrive	Understanding how this millstone works, and what tools can get us out from under	What steps can we take now? What more must we learn?

Models of Response and Resistance

51a

From Privilege, Activism

Asked how people raised in privilege could hope to be good activists, organizer/educator Marshall Ganz replied:

"Wasn't Moses raised in Pharaoh's house?"

-- From a 2015 Facebook crowd-sourcing: Joelle Novey, DC area
   Ganz is senior lecturer at Harvard's Kennedy School of Government;
   former staff of United Farm Workers, political trainer and campaigner

Vision and Action

At least one *Yisrael-ite*, Yocheved, launches her child into the Nile to evade the death-order for male babies. This shows some degree of faith in her *Mitzrayim-ite* neighbors, trusting that someone will rescue the child that she cannot raise because of the edict. Moreover, at least one *Mitzrayim-ite*, Pharaoh's daughter (named Batya, in midrash), does in fact rescue a child from the Nile, also refusing to dehumanize the other, and recognizing the humanity of the baby and his family.

Perhaps there were more *Yisrael-ites* launching babies into the river and more *Mitzrayim-ites* rescuing them. But even if these two women were unique in their world, their example teaches that some on either side of a class-divide or conflict can see humanity in the other.... and that such vision is necessary for the overturning of oppression.

-- based loosely on a sermon at Tifereth Israel in Columbus OH, 2016

Is This Resistance?

In contrast to the many small acts of women who appear early in Exodus (and then largely disappear), Moses' first act as an adult, a big dramatic one, did nothing -- to all appearances in the text and commentary -- to overturn oppression in the long run and illustrates one danger of dehumanizing actors in an oppressive system. (Exodus 2)

Over the centuries, many explanations have been offered for Moses' killing of the *Mitzrayim-ite*, most seeking to justify him (many by imputing cruel capital offenses to the man he killed), some calling Moses out for anger or immaturity, and others identifying this action as the reason Moses later dies without entering the Land (cannot find a source for this, and I've asked around with no success; so perhaps I remembered wrong).

Leaving commentary aside for now, let's look at the action and the language of the text itself:

- Moses "had grown up" (in the palace) and now meets his kinsfolk/kinsmen (the Hebrew means "brothers");

- Moses' very first act in the world of his "brothers," is a violent one;

- Moses' attempt to mediate between or judge his own people is rebuffed;

- "Then the matter is known!" is sometimes interpreted to mean the *Yisrael-ites* were informants;

- Whatever the reasons for his behavior, the result for Moses is his own mini-exile.

A stranger to one's brothers, now estranged from one's upbringing, immersed in confusing and dangerous politics with no one to help navigate. How common is this circumstance!
-- inspired in part by (long ago) Torah discussions at Fabrangen Havurah

Is THIS Resistance?

Just two verses after the above drama, Moses, a complete stranger to Midian, helps unknown sisters water their flocks amid harassment:

Is this a model of standing up for justice no matter what?

Or is it an interloper instantly intervening, for better or worse, in a local power struggle, possibly destabilizing the neighborhood?

One lesson to take away from the young adulthood of Moses might simply be how pervasive and complex is the effect of that millstone and how difficult it is to act with any efficacy within an oppressive system.... especially on one's own....

School for Departure

Passover can be approached as an experience of the ability and power to change anything -- beginning with the switch from fermented products to Passover's unleavened diet:

Think of a fire drill: Where is your exit? And where will everyone meet up once you all get out?

Passover is like a fire drill, because we still have oppressive situations in our world, and we all need to be ready for life saving actions.
-- 2010 Passover preparation blog, Amy Brookman, DC area

In a similar vein, the Highlander Folk School, founded in 1932, has helped incubate grassroots organizing, from desegregation in the labor movement, through the Montgomery bus boycott, to prison justice in Central Appalachian today. The school brings together participants often separated in the outside world, due to legal or de facto segregation, and offers inter-generational opportunities to refine thinking, hone skills, and develop a community similarly committed to the essential, perhaps dangerous, work ahead. In these ways, Highlander Education and Research Center serves as a model "school for departure" to inspire new approaches to joint liberation.

Perhaps Moses' Midian stay was also a "school for departure," under the guidance of his new family: his wife Zipporah, who is apparently able to face down God to save her family (see the weird incident at the lodging, Exodus 4:24-26), and his father-in-law Jethro, who later helps turn chaos into a system of community justice (Exodus 18).

Crossers-Over

Pharaoh gives midwives Shifra and Puah a direct order to kill *Yisrael-ite* baby boys. They refuse and have a story ready (more on this later) when he summons them again, demanding to know why they defied him.

We meet the midwives in Exodus 1:15. The expression describing them -- *m'yalleldot* [midwives] *ha-ivriyot* [Hebrew] -- is ambiguous in Hebrew: It can mean either "Hebrews who are midwives" or "midwives to the Hebrews." Given the context, it seems that the latter reading would mean *Mitzrayim-ites* serving *Yisrael-ite* women in birthing. Both possibilities are oft-pursued.

Resisting Conventions

There is a lesson here, however the phrase is parsed: The word "Hebrew [*ivrit*]" probably comes from the root for "crossing over," and the midwives, whatever their background, live up to that name:

> ...it might be said that no matter their origins, they were in their essence Ivriyot. These courageous women were at odds with their surroundings much as Abraham and other Ivrim in the Bible were at odds with theirs. As we have seen, the prevailing culture in Egypt imposes its conformity among oppressors and oppressed alike. The oppressed are cowed into a state of silent suffering, and the oppressors become gradually inured to the degradation and ultimately to to the murder of unwanted foreigners. The midwives stand as Ivriyot, steadfastly resisting the corrupt conventions that have taken hold of their society.
> -- Judy Klitsner, *Subversive Sequels in the Bible*, p.58

Pharaoh summons midwives who are already at work among *Yisrael-ite* women. Given how unlikely it would be for only two midwives to attend so many births, some commentary sees Shifrah and Puah as "head midwives," with many underlings. So what was going on with all these midwives?

- Perhaps Shifrah and Puah were part of a large, oppressive welfare-type system, of a piece with the taskmasters.

  - Maybe they'd been going along to get along, in a tough system, and then had a change of heart when Pharaoh demanded outright baby killing.

  - Maybe they had always been doing their best to keep the midwives they supervised from dehumanizing mothers and babies in their care, "resisting the corrupt conventions of their society."

- Then again, maybe, just maybe, they were part of a whole network of genuine crossers-over, *Yisrael-ites* and *Mitzrayim-ites* who never bought into palace propaganda.

  (the kernel of this teaching is from a participant-led session of "Kol Isha," a group which explored spirituality from a woman's perspective for many years at Temple Micah, DC; early 2000s.)

Reparations

51b

Exodus and Reparations

As the battle between God and Pharaoh comes to a close, there is an exchange of treasure between the *Mitzrayim-ites* and the *Yisrael-ites*:

> The Israelites had done Moses' bidding and asked from the *Mitzrayim-ites* objects of silver and gold, and clothing. And YHVH had disposed the *Mitzrayim-ites* favorably toward the people, and they let them have their request; thus they *va-y'natzlu* the Egyptians.
> -- Exodus 12:35-36

The verb used for this exchange, *va-y'natzlu*, is variously translated as "strip away, plunder" or "rescue, deliver," and there are many ways of explaining what happened and why. This text is sometimes used to support the concept of Reparations.

Another discussion of Exodus 12:35-36 argues that the *Yisrael-ites* were owed money from *Mitzrayim-ites* for past labor.

Centuries of treasure-related commentary also link Joseph's actions at the close of Genesis with enslavement in Exodus, raising some questions worth considering in the context of coalition and redemption:

- Joseph helped pharaoh take advantage of famine conditions, amassing wealth from around the world and even taking land and means of livelihood from the people in exchange for food. Whose, in that light, is that treasure?

- What lessons might be drawn for the need for Reparations for people descended from enslaved populations in the United States?

Talmud and Reparations

One year, in a Svara class led by Laynie Solomon, we looked at "the stolen beam" discussion in Babylonian Talmud Gitten 55a. The text speaks about what measures should be taken to compensate the owner, if the stolen beam has been already built into a large structure.

It seemed pretty clear, from the earliest classes, that the rabbis of the Talmud assume the beam had a legitimate owner and was taken, illegitimately. But I was completely stymied by the idea, proposed by Beit Shammai, of returning the beam to it's *"baalav"* — which seems to mean, on the face of it, the beam's "(true) owners." In Modern Hebrew, *"baal habayit* [master of the house]" is a landlord, and I couldn't shake the feeling that some shady landlord was somehow benefiting from a loophole in the law…as too many of our big ones here in DC are wont to do…and had, by vague analogy, no right to that beam in the first place.

Just prior to these studies, I had interviewed advocates for the "Vacant to Virus Reduction" (V2VR) campaign discussed above. One of the arguments of this campaign is that WE, District taxpayers in this use of "we," have already paid dearly for luxury housing — through tax incentives and other perfectly legal means — and so should be able to claim some of that benefit now, in this crisis involving health and housing.

Here in DC, we have thousands of housing insecure people. The DC government regularly removes and destroys the belongings and shelters of neighbors in the encampments, insisting that they have no right to live where they do. The argument for this "cleaning" (a terrifying word) is sometimes that the sidewalks must be unblocked; the same sidewalks will soon be blocked by cafe tables -- or, in a sadder irony: tents! -- to support restaurants. The same DC government regularly supports the building of luxury dwellings with all kinds of incentives which come from taxpayers' pockets.

> ### Gittin 55a: That Stolen Beam
>
> Here is a translation of the relevant verses in Gittin 55a based loosely on what's at Sefaria and our Svara class:
>
>> And about a stolen beam that was built into a large [maybe multi-residential] building [*bira*], remove the value, due to an ordinance instituted for the penitent….Beit Shammai say: He must destroy the entire building and return the beam to its owners [*l'baalav*]…

The Root of the Trouble

Svara method in Talmud study emphasizes looking up each word encountered, even if the study partners think they already know it. We learned that the Hebrew word *"baal,"* which is usually translated as "owner" or "master," is based on a two-letter root, *bet-ayin*. And that root can mean to search out, lay bare, or ransack.

And, while I confess to some bias here before I opened the dictionary, finding this root really spoke to one of the many issues bothering me about the idea of returning the beam to its *baalav*. I cannot honestly argue that either

Beit Shammai or Beit Hillel thought property ownership was a form of ransacking. But I will argue that people in DC, and probably in many other locales, need to be thinking

- about how many of our beams were obtained,

- what it would mean to extract them or their value, and

- whether someone who took a beam — or chose to shelter under one that does not technically belong to them — is really the culprit.

None of this even begins to consider the issue of reparations for the Atlantic Slave Trade, for this country's genocide and massive theft from indigenous people, or for the more recent, ongoing displacement of Black people in DC and elsewhere. But it has caused me to ponder some aspects of the work ahead…

Rescue Me! You! Us!

51c

R' Benno Jacob (see "Scattered," above) presented a view of *Mitzrayim* in which *Mitzrayim-ites* and *Yisrael-ites* had been friendly toward one another, were turned against one another by Pharaoh's propaganda, and then parted with on good terms with gifts (Ex 11:2). Jacob argues that *Mitzrayim-ites'* parting gifts

> were a clear public protest against the policies of the royal tyrant. They demonstrated a renewal of public conscience...a moral change.
> -- Jacob, *The Second Book of the Bible*, p. 343

A contemporary commentary on this reading confesses skepticism as to whether R' Jacob's analysis jives with the plain sense of the text but adds:

> One senses in Jacob's words the insights of a brilliant exegete but also the pain of a rabbi and teacher in a Germany consumed by hate*....In a world suffused with bigotry and hostility, a world in which people of faith often marshal sacred texts to legitimate acts of cruelty and to extol hatred as a virtue, there is great power in reading Jacob's words and being reminded: At the heart of the religious enterprise is the attempt to soften, and open, one's heart, to God and to one-another. If even [*Mitzrayim-ites*] and [*Yisrael-ites*] can be (successfully!) called to love one-another, then perhaps, even in the darkest of times, slim glimmers of hope are available to us.
> -- Held, Shai. "Receiving Gifts (and Learning to Love?): The 'Stripping' of the Egyptians."
> 2015 dvar torah, available via Mechon Hadar

*Held includes a footnote citing personal communication with R. Walter Jacob (Benno's son) to confirm that his father was working on the Exodus commentary between 1934 and 1939, while still in Germany.

On the one hand, I am all for seeking positive messages along our *Rereading Exodus* journey. I endorse Shai Held's lesson: "...even in the darkest of times, slim glimmers of hope are available to us." On the other hand, I fear falling into what I think of as the we're-all-in-this-together, let's-hold-hands-and-march trap.

It is true that all of our liberations -- like those of the *Yisrael-ites* and the *Mitzrayim-ites* -- are bound together. But that doesn't mean that everyone's experiences -- pre-, midst-, and post-liberation -- are equivalent. That millstone that is *Mitzrayim* may be affecting all who are part of an oppressive system, but that doesn't mean the weight is the same on all involved.

On the other other hand, Jews have traditions teaching that the divine is in exile with the People and so in need of rescue, too. This does not make divine and human experiences equivalent either. It does suggest, though, that maybe we're back to the first other hand, and ought to make this "all-in-this-together" thing work for us.

Rescue Yourself and Us!

Jewish prayers begging for rescue and mercy often take the format, "You helped them; help us." An unusual prayer, attributed to Eleazar Kallir (c.570–c.640 CE), implies that God needs saving, too.

The prayer is translated as something like "Save Yourself and us" or "I and You, may You deliver us both," or "Please rescue me and the divine name" [*Ani Va-ho*]. It includes a chorus of "Yourself and us!" and verses describing God accompanying the People out of *Mitzrayim* and other exiles: "As You rescued the communities You exiled to Babylonia, and Your merciful Presence accompanied them — so save us."

This prayer's line of thought, which has been developing for centuries, is mean to teach that "when there is suffering in the world, God is not on the side of the oppressors. Rather God is with the oppressed and suffers with them" (*Or Hadash: A Commentary on Siddur Sim Shalom*).

"Safety" Cards

The idea that "God is with the oppressed" is too often, I fear, used as a sort of universal *Coup-fourré* card, a "safety" to correct any "hazard," so as to stay on the road.

...For those who never played the card game Mille Borne, maybe "ace in the hole" or "Get out of jail free" card will make more sense; but I find *Coup-fourré* — the process whereby one is able to surmount a pitfall and keep rolling along — more apt here....

It is way too easy to let "God is with the oppressed" console the already comfortable while leaving the afflicted with their travails.

On this *Rereading Exodus* journey, all of us must examine our "safety" cards. We must ask ourselves where we are when there is suffering and injustice in the world. If the divine went into exile with us, and something similar is required of us, if we are to make any progress on joint liberation.

> Jewish history presents abundant examples of our communities mistrusting and fearing State forces: from ancient Rome, through Medieval Europe, the Pale of Settlement, pogroms, ghettos -- there were reasons for that Golem -- to the mid-20th Century.
>
> Today many in U.S. Jewish communities view our safety as State-protec-ted, regardless of history. Meanwhile, we might know that such protection is hardly universal: not extended equally to homeless, queer, transgender, mentally ill, black, brown, "foreign," and many other people. Somehow, we barely register the inequity.

We must take steps to remove any sense that we are somehow entitled to dwell in safety when others cannot. If God could join us in exile, we can work to dismantle White Supremacy and other protections that can never be equally shared.

If we believe that "God is not to be found on the side of the oppressors," we had better consider where we are standing ourselves.

If we are going to come out of this Exodus experience knowing something new, we have to being by understanding where we are.

Thank you for joining this journey.

Thank you for supporting Charnice Milton Community Bookstore.

Stay in touch via rereading4liberation.com and weluvbooks.org

-- Virginia Avniel Spatz

DC March 2022/Adar Bet 5782

Bibliography

Hebrew Bible/Tanakh:

Jewish Publication Society 1917, available on Mechon-Mamre.org
JPS 1985, available on Sefaria.org
Alter, Robert. *The Five Books of Moses*. NY: Norton, 1995
Fox, Everett Fox. *The Five Books of Moses*. NY: Schocken, 1995

The Peoples' Companion to the Bible, Fortress Press, 2010. DeYoung, Gafney, Guardiola-Saenz, Tinker, and Yamada, eds.

Torah: A Women's Commentary. Union for Reform Judaism, 2008.

Books

Asch, Chris Myers and George Derek Musgrove.
    Chocolate City: A History of Race and Democracy in the Nation's Capital.
    Chapel Hill: Univ of North Carolina Press, 2017.

Cassuto, Umberto. *A commentary on the Book of Exodus*.
    Jerusalem: Magnes Press, 1997; first Hebrew 1951

Davis, Angela Y. "Speech delivered at the Embassy Auditorium 1972,"
    IN *Say It Loud!: Great Speeches on Civil Rights and African American Identity*.
    Editors: Catherine Ellis, Stephen Drury Smith. NY: the New Press, 2010

Dollinger, Marc. *Black Power, Jewish Politics*.
    Waltham, MA: Brandeis Univ., 2018

Foer, Jonathan Safran, ed. *New American Haggadah*.
    Boston: Little Brown, 2012. Translation by Nathan Englander.

Gregory, Dick. *Dick Gregory's Bible Tales with Commentary*
    James R. McGraw, ed. NY: Stein and Day, 1974.

Heschel, Abraham Joshua. Conference on "RELIGION AND RACE" (14
    JANUARY 1963). Proceedings published as booklet.
    Also available online at University of Maryland, among other sites

Heschel, A. J. Susannah Heschel, ed.
    Moral Grandeur and Spiritual Audacity. NY: Farrar, Straus, Giroux, 1996.

Hopkinson, Natalie. *Go-Go Live: The Musical Live and Death of a Chocolate
    City*. Durham, NC: Duke Univ Press, 2012

Hurston, Zora Neale. *Moses, Man of the Mountain*. NY: Harper, 1991
    (originally published 1939)

Ignatiev, Noel. *How the Irish Became White*. Routledge, 1996.

Jacob, Benno. Jacob, Walter and Yaakov Elman, trans. *The Second Book of the Bible: Exodus, Interpreted by Benno Jacob.*Hoboken, NJ: Ktav, 1992

King, Martin Luther, Jr. *Where Do We Go From Here: Chaos or Community?* 1967; Reprinted, Boston: Beacon Press, 2010

Klitsner, Judy. *Subversive Sequels in the Bible: How Biblical Stories Mine and Undermine Each Other.* Jerusalem: Maggid Books/Koren, 2011

Lornell, Kip and Charles C. Stephenson. *The Beat: Go-Go's Fusion of Funk and Hip-Hop. Columbus:* Univ. Press of Mississippi, 2009

MaNishtana (R' Shais Rishon). *Fine, thanks, how are you, Jewish?* Create Space, 2014.

Magee, Rhonda V. *The Inner Work of Racial Justice: Healing Ourselves and Transforming Our Communities through Mindfulness.* NY: TarcherPerigee (Penguin Random House), 2019.

Ostriker, Alicia Suskin. *Nakedness of the Fathers.* New Brunswick, NJ: Rutgers University Press, 1997. Includes "The Nursing Father"

powell, john a. *Racing to Justice: Transforming Our Conceptions of Self and Other to Build an Inclusive Society.* Bloomington: Indiana Univ Press, 2012

Silber, David. "Rereading the Plagues," IN *Go Forth and Learn: A Passover Haggadah.* Philadelphia, PA: JPS, 2011

Russell, Thaddeus. *A Renegade History of the United States.* Free Press, 2010

Summers, Brandi Thompson. *Black in Place: The Spatial Aesthetics of Race in a Post-Chocolate City.* Chapel Hill: Univ of North Carolina Press, 2019

Articles/PDFs/Speeches

David, Justin. "Benevolent Dictatorship or Righteous Balance?" at MyJewishLearning.com

Ford, Glen. "No Compromise, No Retreat in the Fight to End Militarism and War," Keynote Address, Black Alliance for Peace, April 4, 2019 on BAP Facebook page -- available without FB account

Harris, Cheryl I. "Whiteness as Property," Harvard Law Review, 2006.

Held, Shai. "Receiving Gifts (and Learning to Love?): The 'Stripping' of the Egyptians." 2015 dvar torah, available via Mechon Hadar

JFREJ. *#BLM Haggadah Supplement,* 2016. Jews for Racial & Economic Justice. look for "JFREJ Haggadah Library" at www.jfrej.org

JFREJ. *Understanding Antisemitism: An Offering to Our Movement,* A Resource from Jews for Racial & Economic Justice, 2017. www.jfrej.org

JFREJ. *Unraveling Antisemitism and Discussion Guide, 2022.*
https://www.jfrej.org/campaigns/antisemitism

King, Martin Luther, Jr. "Remaining Awake Through a Great Revolution,"
National Cathedral, 3/31/68. Text at King Institute at Stanford.
Recordings also widely available.

Lappe, Benay. "The Crash Talk," Svara: A Traditionally Radical Yeshiva.
https://svara.org/crash/

Moskovitz, Daniel. "Pharaoh Didn't Know Joseph," commentary provided
by Union for Reform Judaism, at MyJewishLearning.com

Orlow, Avi. "Modeling Respect on Lag B'Omer" on behalf of Keshet: For
LGBTQ Equality in Jewish Life, 4/19/2013 MyJewishLearning.com

Rabbinical Assembly. *Or Hadash: A commentary on Siddur Sim Shalom's festival
supplement.* Available for download from Rabbinical Assembly website

Rowlands, D.W. "How household incomes in the D.C. area have changed
since 1980." DC Policy Center (www.dcpolicycenter.org)

Sojourner, Sabrina. "Some are Guilty, but All are Responsible," remarks on
Kabbalat Shabbat at Kol Shalom (Rockville, MD).
SabrinaSojourner.net

Spatz, V. "Toward a Jews' Self-Inventory for Bible Readers," is available on
"A Song Every Day" blog and at Academia.edu.

Urban Institute. *The Color of Wealth in the Nation's Capital*, 2016

More

"DC 101" -- Serve Your City/Ward 6 Mutual Aid
Cited here: "Housing and Development" and "Health"
www.facebook.com/ServeYourCityDC/videos

"Project Orange Tree" at https://pottest.wordpress.com
DNAinfo.com story, March 2013, tinyurl.com/mu925vjz

V2VR.info -- Vacancy to Virus Reduction

www.ingramcontent.com/pod-product-compliance
Lightning Source LLC
Chambersburg PA
CBHW022333280326
41934CB00006B/625